Ecommerce 2.0

This edition published 2007

Imano plc	Imano inc
198 High Holborn	27 West 20th Street
London WC1V 7BD	New York 10011
United Kingdom	USA
Telephone: 020 7632 6930	Telephone: 646 442 4416
Email: experts@imano.com	Email: us.experts@imano.com
www.imano.com	www.imano.com

ISBN 978-0-9549055-4-5

Contents

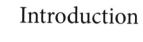

Introduction

Why Ecommerce 2.0?

At its inception, everybody was learning about the web. Optimism and great ideas were abundant, but in the midst of all the excitement, longevity was vastly overlooked. Huge investments went into these ideas with people expecting returns in months. The reality was that they needed to wait years. The early pioneers and great ideologists are the predecessors of today's billion dollar companies like Google, YouTube and LinkedIn. In 2001, the optimism that started the web revolution diminished, as the reality that *'remaining sustainable required profits'* permeated, and subsequently thousands of great ideas failed.

Now the landscape has changed. Some of the great ideas never disappeared. Some ideas just evolved. And the growth of internet usage and its impact on behaviour have now made it viable for companies to make money. For those that have been there from the beginning, we have seen structure out of chaos, knowledge out of information and sustainability out of hype. To define this new era the term Web 2.0 was born and from those same principles we give you Ecommerce 2.0.

The early days of ecommerce were just about being able to find a product and pay for it online and sometimes even that was a challenge. Companies focused on using the internet as a lower cost channel without the need for retail or call-centre staff. However, the reality was that ecommerce required substantial learning and infrastructure to be put into place, which meant a significant investment had to be made. Most online stores were little more than a bad version of a paper catalogue. However, things have changed. Ecommerce 2.0 is about offering much more than a paper catalogue or a retail experience. With ecommerce, you can now search through the text of books on Amazon, you can share reviews and ratings, tag your favourite products, be guided through attributes to find the item that meets your exact specification. Products like apparel and furniture that were initially regarded as being the least likely categories to sell online have become the fastest growing areas. The in-store touch and feel experience has been replicated by online visualisation tools. Ecommerce 2.0 is about engaging the consumer with an exceptional shopping experience. It is about letting consumers be social. It is about delivering more than could have ever been delivered through catalogues or in-store.

We have split the book into four main chapters that form the core of the evolution of ecommerce. **Marketing 2.0** looks at the essence of marketing, influencing customer behaviour and encompasses both old and new media. **Social 2.0** considers social networking and its tools to provide significant value beyond standard ecommerce. **Engage 2.0** focuses on the customer and delivering each one a fantastic experience. Finally, **Channel 2.0** considers the channel integration from the customer's perspective and how to overcome some of the current issues with multi-channel pricing and promotions.

Why Marketing 2.0

Marketing 2.0 provides a different outlook to marketing practice, moving away from an advertising driven '*What media can I buy?*' approach to a much more successful '*How can I best influence my customer to purchase?*' It relies on a strong understanding of your customers and their buying cycle. It considers who the right kind of customer is and how best to influence them. The Marketing 2.0

model goes beyond advertising and considers other opportunities that can best influence the customer, like online configurator tools and call-centre optimisation. In addition, Marketing 2.0 considers behavioural marketing campaigns, which are triggered by specific customer activity to deliver timely and effective communication with a strong return.

Why Social 2.0

Groups of people have always been powerful at changing the world, from unions to political groups. Now with the Internet, a community of people online influences the way people and corporations react. Harnessing the community by using online social tools, has changed the face of ecommerce and is likely to have an even greater impact in the coming years. Social 2.0 covers the principles of social networking, the social tools from forums to wikis and enabler technologies like web services.

Why Engage 2.0

Delivering a wonderful consumer experience is Engage 2.0. A customer expects much more than the bare minimum ecommerce functionality, thus, utilising advanced tools for delivering and managing the customers experience are vital. In this chapter, we look at the key drivers to engage the consumer from advanced loyalty to search and customer experience management as a model for making sure your customers are happy.

Why Channel 2.0

Looking at ecommerce returns in terms of online revenue is shortsighted and does not reflect the true power of multi-channel integration. From the huge amount of influence the internet has on pre-purchase research to the power of seamless interaction across channels, Channel 2.0 is about each channel embracing and enhancing each other. In this chapter, we discuss synchronising pricing, promotions, marketing, gift vouchers, orders and returns using tools that give you a single view of the customer.

This book is written with the view to aid practitioners in understanding the impact, the evolution of ecommerce and marketing will have on their organisations. The ideas and concepts discussed within this book will provide a real competitive advantage. The companies that embrace **Ecommerce 2.0** will see their businesses flourish!

Marketing 2.0

Marketing 2.0

Marketing has evolved, it has grown up. The days when you could reach 60% of the population by running a TV advert on primetime are long over. Now there is a huge fragmentation of media with new marketing opportunities appearing every few months, while existing ones like the humble billboard have evolved into interactive mediums, allowing people to touch digital screens and download content. Traditional advertising practice focuses on identifying potential customers' demographic profile, giving age groups, gender, and earnings, and then matching this with media that has a similar demographic profile. This approach does not take into account the unique measurability and interactivity of new media.

Companies have been slow to take on new media opportunities without an appropriate framework to assess their success. They have relied on replicating past successes, even with the recent radical change in consumer behaviour, which has seen consumers spending 34% of their time online but marketers only spending 6% of their budget.[1] Procter & Gamble GMO Jim Stengel sums it up, "*Marketing is a $450 billion industry, and we are all making decisions with less data and discipline than we apply to $100,000 decisions in other aspects of our business.*"

Marketing 2.0 is about better understanding customers through behavioural and attitudinal research in addition to standard demographics. It is about creating key customer personas and not about working off a generalised view of the customer that we are all too familiar with. How many times have we heard companies saying *our customers are age 25-35, primarily female, with incomes of £15-24,000 per annum*. What about the customers that fall outside these broad profiles? Marketing 2.0 is about understanding who your valuable customers are. Current marketing thinking looks at *what media to buy*, Marketing 2.0 every stage in the buying cycle and looks at what options will best influence the customer to purchase, whether it is advertising or a new online product finder tool. Marketing 2.0 is not about an annual marketing review, it is about continual optimisation through analytics, A/B testing and marketing mix models, which all help generate a bigger bang for the buck. The concepts behind Marketing 2.0 are proven to deliver exceptional results, with Ford projecting an additional $90 million in revenue just by moving 2% of the marketing budget to online.

In this chapter, we outline the problems with traditional marketing and illustrate *how to understand*, who your customers are, how to find your most valuable customers, how to get more of these ideal customers and how to optimize your marketing. With a Marketing 2.0 model you will have a better understanding of how new technology can be incorporated into your marketing mix and how you can achieve significantly better results without additional budget.

The Trouble with Marketing

There are significant issues with the current marketing model that has led many marketers to achieve results, which are below par with campaigns that do not fulfil the promises they set out too. The problems with the current marketing practise are:

1. Relying on using tried and tested marketing strategies, which do not adapt well to work with the new online landscape.
2. It does little to help provide an understanding of how to exploit new technologies for success.
3. Focusing on advertising opportunities, rather than changing consumer behaviour.
4. Rely on ineffectual marketing segmentation that does little to help understand customers and how to influence their behaviour.
5. Does not look at non-standard marketing options like call-centre, ecommerce or retail optimisation, which could have the greatest impact on converting people to paying customers.
6. Marketing spend allocation is often based on historical campaigns and what media was available to buy.
7. More of an art relying on gut feeling rather than science and data.
8. Plans are often left completely in the hands of an advertising agency who allocate budget based on their channel expertise and what is most profitable for them. Why should they experiment with new online channels where they have little or no experience and they know that it will generate proportionally smaller revenue compared to their core marketing activities?
9. Some marketing planners have continued to run campaigns that have little changed over the years, whilst consumers' actual channel usage and behaviour has changed considerably in recent years.
10. It does not consider quick-win behavioural triggered marketing.

11. Allocation of budget per channel is often arbitrary and not in-line with consumer behaviour.
12. Typically, budgets are only revisited annually. Unspent budget is often taken away.
13. Rarely focused on true return-on-investment.
14. Focuses on reach and frequency rather influencing customer behaviour.
15. Uses metrics like reach and Gross Rating Points (GRP) which are traditionally TV metrics and do not work well with newer media.
16. Does not consider the intertwining of sales channels, like in-store kiosks.
17. Does not consider social networking opportunities.

For all the pains of marketing, Marketing 2.0 is the remedy.

Understanding Your Customers

Customer Centric

At the core of Marketing 2.0 is a data driven holistic view of your customers rather than generalised profiles. A customer centric approach considers more than demographics and builds detailed customer profiles using behaviour and attitudinal data. Customer centric is knowing the customer buying cycle from awareness to post-purchase and understanding what options from advertising to checkout optimisation will best influence the customer's behaviour along the buying cycle. Being customer-centric is about having a single view of the customer and considering them in every action throughout the organisation from product development right through to post-purchase product support. Customer centric organisations always look at things from the customer's perspective and want continually to surpass their customer's expectations.

Where to Gather Data From

A customer centric approach is considerably easier in today's age of data warehousing and loyalty programs. Every consumer can be individually identified and campaigns created exclusively for each consumer. You can build up detailed customer profile using:

- Purchases
- Surveys
- Call-centre calls
- Email correspondence
- Interactions with online marketing
- Web site usage
- Forums
- Feedback and comments
- Product reviews and ratings
- Vouchers and promotions redeemed
- Text mining data. Text based communication like email, reviews, comments and forum entries are often only referred to when there is a specific customer issue but with text mining techniques, structured data can be generated from this content.
- Calculated insight data from predictive analysis. Predictive analysis is the generation of a computer model, using customer data, to gain insight through patterns in data (covered in more depth in the Predictive Analysis section later in this chapter).

Collect Demographics

Demographic data is often the easiest to collect and consists of:

- Age
- Gender
- Ethnicity
- Geographic location
- Level of education
- Income
- Socioeconomic status
- Religion
- Marital status
- Size of family
- Ownership (home, car, pet, etc.)
- Language
- Life cycles (fertility, mortality, migration)

Traditional marketing focuses on generating average or ranges of customer demographic that was then matched with the target demographic of publication or channel where you were looking to advertise. The criticism of average demographic profiles is that it relies on generalisations that never reflect any real person within the segment. With Marketing 2.0, we look at individual demographic profiles and add behavioural and attitudinal data to gain real customer insight.

Collect Behavioural Data

Behavioural data is often collected in operational activity and often needs to be collated from various sources and aggregated. Behavioural data per customer can consist of:

- Purchasing and order information
- Searches on the web site or viewing a particular section
- Items added to a shopping basket
- Support request
- Interest in products or brand through survey responses
- Email requests

In the behavioural marketing section, we look at other behaviours that can be used for marketing.

Collect Attitudinal Data

Attitudinal data is collected using surveys and theses surveys are often online but can be in-person or via the telephone. Defining the attitudes that are important relies on asking relevant and useful questions that can help build strong insight into the customer's attitudes. The kind of questions that you need to ask is based on the products or service you sell and the gravity of the purchasing decision the customer needs to make.

Gravity of Customer Decision

Not all purchases are equal. Some shallow decisions have little impact on a consumer's life, like buying toilet roll or a new deodorant. If the consumer did not like the item, they would just not purchase it next time. While others are middle decisions, buying a car for most people is a big purchase and would be carefully considered – a mistake in this purchasing decision would be longer lived. With the deepest decisions involving life changing choices, like where to live or a particular medical treatment. Looking at the gravity of a decision, you can start to understand what the consumer's concerns are and what attitudinal information you should be looking to identify.

Gravity of decision	Consumer purchase	Attitudes to survey
Shallow decision	Functional items	Price elasticity Brand loyalty Usage behaviour Quality/value for money
Middle decision	Cars, Some electronics Holidays	Lifestyle Social status Self-image Better meets needs Better functionality/features
Deep decisions	Home location Medical treatment	Core consumer values and beliefs

Generating Personas

Every customer is unique but targeting media uniquely to every customer is often impossible. Rather than fall into the catch-all flaw of a single generic demographic profile, a better methodology is persona marketing. A persona is a fictional customer that is an archetype of each of your customer segments who share similar attitudes and goals. You would typically have 2-7 personas depending on the diversity of your customer base and select one persona as your focal persona, which will always be the primary consideration when validating key marketing. Personas should be accurate representations of customers founded on sound ethnographic research and should look and sound like the people they represent and not fall into being stereotypes. These personas are used to make decisions against and validate marketing campaigns against ensuring that everything is considered from a customer's perspective. For each persona, you create a page of narrative with photographs and detailed information including name, age, habits, interests, motivations and goals that you derive from your demographic, behavioural and attitudinal research.

The key strengths of creating effective personas are:

1. That it encourages people to look at things from a customer's perspective but more than that, it helps your team live and breath from the persona's perspective.
2. That it encourages design for the persona that you can visualise rather than an average demographic. It is certainly easier to see if a campaign or particular site design will work for Sarah rather a female, age 25-30.
3. Focuses on motivations and behaviors typical of a broad range of users, while still relating to each persona as an individual.
4. It focuses attention on key customer segments.

5. It focuses your marketing campaigns. For instance, *will SMS be appropriate for your oldest persona?*
6. It helps determine what features or functionality will be most appropriate.
7. It lets you understand the customer throughout their buying process so you can best influence a customer's behaviour.
8. It helps create shared vocabulary between the customer and the company so communication can be relevant and clear.
9. It lets companies quickly create value from market research. Newly generated market research can lead to a persona being amended or created and quickly be translated to marketing validation.
10. They give an insight into customers far beyond traditional approaches, which let the marketing team make better decisions.
11. They help identify potential opportunities in marketing that may not have been previously considered. For instance, Crest marketed its toothpaste in nightclubs and bars with an 'Irresistibility IQ' SMS quiz.

For each persona, we can define a set of goals and scenarios to help validate designs and campaigns against. In a company where persona marketing is central to the organisation, people can often talk about whether this campaign would work for Joe or not. Companies that embrace persona marketing have created rooms where marketers can immerse themselves to understand more about that persona from items like books, CD's and products in the room.

As much of Marketing 2.0 is about validating your marketing against personas, it is essential to get the persona creation process right. To create personas you need to:

1. Analyse customer data to define your key customer groups by looking at standard demographic information and behavioural information. Using this data 2-7 customer groups should be able to be identified. If you have more then it is quite likely that some groups can be merged together because their behaviour or attitudes are likely to be similar.
2. With these groups, you need to build an attitudinal profile to understand what motivates these consumers. You can do this by surveying members of each group. This can be done through surveys online, on the telephone or in person.

Combine this data to build accurate personas that define demographic, behavioural and attitudinal information.

Identifying Your Most Valuable Customers

To understanding which customers are most valuable to your business, you need to look at a number of metrics that include:
- Profitability
- Orders
- Support requests
- Returns
- Acquisition costs
- Retention costs
- Length of time that they remain a customer

These factors together produce a true customer lifetime value, which then can help understand which customers are valuable to the business and in turn help you find more.

Customers are more likely to be valuable, if they:

- Buy high margin products
- Place a few large orders rather than many small orders
- Make no order amendments, returns or support request
- Pay on-time
- Pay full price without negotiating discounts
- Stay as customers for longer
- Acquisition costs are lower
- Retention costs are lower
- Make positive recommendations (promoters)

This data should not be looked at independently but in unison as one factor often affects another, for instance customers who have low acquisition costs are also quite likely to be customers for a shorter period. In the following matrix, we have identified four different segments based on acquisition and retention costs and can see that the most valuable 'Royal' customer segment will have originated from the highest cost acquisitions and retention marketing.[2]

	Low **Acquisition Cost** High
High Maintenance Customers	**Royal Customers**
Casual Customers (largest segment)	**Low Maintenance Customers** (tend to be most profitable)

Retention Cost: High / Low

Promoters

Successful companies see a strong correlation between their performance and the number and strength of their customer promoters. The promoter is the customer who is loyal and recommends additional customers to your organisation. To evaluate promoter customers, you could look at customer repeat purchases but this does not provide enough information to understand how loyal customers really are, as a customer with multiple repeat purchases who only buys off you 50% of the time is not necessarily as loyal as a customer that only buys off you a couple of times but doesn't buy off anyone else. According to the *Harvard Business Review* after extensive research the strongest factor for identifying the promoter customer is in response to the survey question *Would you recommend us to a friend or colleague?* Answering this question requires the customer to be willing to put their reputation on the line to recommend you. To obtain the net-promoter score, you ask the question asking customers to score from 0 to 10. The key performance metric is created by subtracting the number of detractors (score 0-6) from the number of promoters (score 9-10). This not only provides a metric that should be circulated throughout the organisation but using segmentation, you can calculate the score from various different marketing activities.[3]

Would you recommend [brand or company x] to a friend or colleague?

0	1	2	3	4	5	6	7	8	9	10
Not likely					Neutral				Extremely likely	
Detractors									Promoters	

Successful organisations like Amazon and eBay have net-promoter scores from 75% to more than 80% and these levels are what organisations should be aiming to achieve. Understanding who your net-promoters are is part of the process of getting additional valuable customers.

How to Get More of Your Ideal Customers

Customer's Stage in Buying Cycle

A customer goes through various different stages in making their purchasing decision from the first point where they are made aware of your brand or product to when they purchase and importantly become loyal repeat customers. At key trigger points in this buying cycle, the customer will be able to be influenced positively to the next stage and ultimately a buying decision. Marketing 2.0 is about looking at these trigger points and understanding the best marketing opportunity which will have the greatest positive influence on the customer's behaviour. For example, a car company may consider different communication at different stages in the buying process:

1. **Early awareness** – TV advertising
2. **Research and pricing** – Web-site car configurator
3. **Test Drive** – Free gift offer
4. **Complete purchase** – Interest free credit communication by direct mail

Customer buying cycle

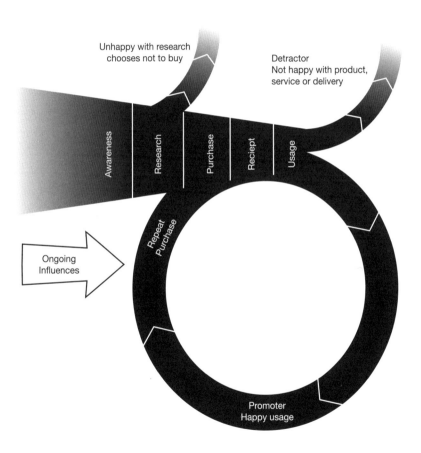

Promotions

Different consumers respond differently to different offers. Where one consumer might be influenced to purchase by a *£5 off voucher*, another consumer may be influenced by a *buy one get one free offer*. Tracking the response to each promotion can help determine which offers are the most likely to appeal to which particular consumers/ personas. Measurement of a promotion by persona against the average will show the most effective promotions at influencing customers.

Conversion of promotion by persona

Promotion	Average	Persona 1	Persona 2	Persona 3
Buy 1 get 1 free	12%	12%	10%	14%
Buy 5 for £50	10%	9%	10%	11%
3 for 2	11%	10%	12%	11%
£5 off when you spend £50	8%	11%	8%	5%

In addition to looking at the short-term affect of promotions, you should consider the long-term implications especially against advertising. Analysing price promotions showed that promotion activity changed the customers' attitudes and they became more price sensitive and started expecting and waiting for a promotion, which leads to a situation where promotions have to be continuously repeated to keep the same market share. On the other hand, advertising tended to reduce price sensitivity, increase loyalty and build brand.[4]

The Influence of Media

Customers are influenced by media from TV to newspapers by varying amounts. This influence is important to Marketing 2.0, as we need consider the most appropriate method marketing options for influencing the customer's behaviour throughout their buying cycle. With the huge fragmentation of media, the impact of any specific piece of media has declined. This media influence per channel can be mapped for each of your personas (see diagram). According to a recent study[5] apart from consumer goods where consumers rely on store and newspaper inserts and banking where consumers like interfacing with a real person consumers ranked web sites as the most important influence on their purchasing decisions with higher ticket items like cars being researched online. This growth in the web's influence and the growth of online social networks are reshaping the allocation of media budgets.

Influence of media on behaviour

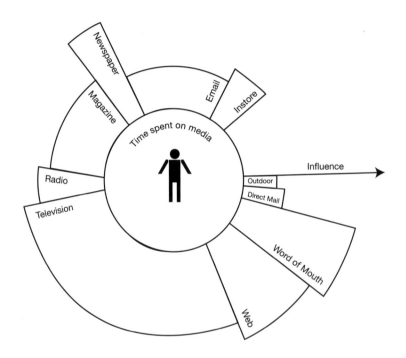

Behaviour Triggered Marketing

With all this marketing communication, a blanket marketing campaign is not necessarily the most appropriate way to reach someone when they are at a specific place in their buying process. A behavioural approach looks at certain patterns in someone's behaviour, and then triggers appropriate communication. One-to-one channels like direct mail and email tend to be more appropriate for behavioural triggered communication whilst newer channels like IPTV are likely to provide additional opportunities. These behaviour-triggered communications have a very strong response rate because they are:

1. uniquely targeted
2. personalised
3. are delivered at a stage in the buying cycle where they can influence the customer's behaviour

Behavioural campaigns are often easy to implement and have a strong return on investment.

Identifying actions that warrant triggers needs to look at the distinct behaviour, the resultant marketing act, the channel and create an ROI estimation to calculate if the event is triggered enough times to justify the creation and management of the communication act. In the following table, we are identify common triggers and possible communication.

Trigger Event	Example Marketing Act	Channel
Customer adds something to their ecommerce shopping basket	Up sell additional items related to the item added to the basket	Ecommerce Site
Fails ecommerce checkout process	Ask if they had problems giving them another opportunity to purchase and offer telephone order service	Email
Birthday	Send birthday card with promotional voucher Advise on setting up a birthday wish list	Email Direct Mail
Buying history	New music album available by an artist you downloaded before	Email Direct Mail SMS
Not purchased for a few months	Survey to ask if something is wrong with an customer re-activation promotion like a discount voucher	Email Direct Mail
Top spending customers	Special thank you with a loyalty promotion	Email Direct Mail SMS
Flights to the same route	Ensure loyalty through special flight promotion and highlight benefits of loyalty programme	Email Direct Mail SMS

Trigger Event	Example Marketing Act	Channel
Countdown to reach next level of membership	Marketing communication showing only two more stays to reach gold status or one more flight to be a platinum member	Email Direct Mail SMS
Global roaming into a new country with a mobile	Message welcoming you to our network with information on directory services	SMS
Mobile/Broadband/ Cable contract about to expire	Marketing communication sowing the virtues of staying with the mobile network and promotional upgrades	Email Direct Mail SMS
Price change on a product	An email alert that informs the customer that the product has now reached their desired price	Email SMS
Visits web site and does not purchase	Deliver advertising just for them on other sites to encourage a return visit and a purchase completion	Banner Advertising

The Integrated Campaign

An often-contested argument is whether a truly integrated campaign exists or could ever exist. The variations of media capabilities make this a truly daunting task. A great idea may translate very well online but may be difficult to put on billboards. Any weakness in the multi-channel communication is quickly picked up by consumers who reject the relationship between the channels and message. To create a truly integrated campaign the idea at inception stage, has to be evaluated against each channel with channel advocates. No idea should be initially rejected but clearly rated against each channel and early concepts outlined. This structured approach will lead to better integrated campaigns whilst marketing channels that will not work can be rejected earlier, rather than trying to re-adapt creative at a later date.

Marketing Channels

With a diversified and expanding set of channels, it is important to understand the implications of particular channels in the media mix. The following section provides an overview of the most popular marketing mechanisms and looks at additional options that influence the customer behaviour. In addition, the marketing channels table provides information on each channel and how well targeted they are, whether they can be driven by cost effective behavioural targeting, entry costs for the media, accuracy of measurement and the common measurement metrics.

Traditional TV Commercials

The 30-second TV slot is still one of the most powerful mediums to reach the mass consumer. TV commercials have become more entertaining to help prevent people channel switching and fast-forwarding them on their Personal Video Recorders (PVR). The increase in the number of TV channels and the fragmentation of media as a whole has meant the days of reaching the mass population with an advert during a primetime show are over. The last few remaining mass reach opportunities, like the US Superbowl, are heavily sought after.

On-Demand/IPTV Commercials

A fast growing space where users can select the programmes they want to see directly either through their computer or set-top boxes. Interstitials that appear before a show starts are the fastest growing format. This is an exciting opportunity, for those that can take advantage of this new medium.

Radio

A great way to reach the car driver. Radio advertising has become more creative to prevent channel switching. London's largest commercial radio station, Capital Radio, has moved to a two-slot radio commercials to discourage channel switching.

Internet Radio

Radio that is delivered over the Internet. Internet radio has the flexibility to allow show sponsorship or in-stream advertising. Last. fm is a pioneer, building a user specific radio station based on music preferences.

Podcasts

With over 30 million Apple iPods and other MP3 devices sold a year, the Podcast has captured the in-transit consumer who instead of wasting travel time, can now listen to entertainment and news. The key for great Podcast is great content.

Traditional Outdoor

Billboards have been around for quite a while but with innovations in digital display technology, they have taken on a new flair showing video and animated adverts.

Interactive Outdoor

Combining technology and outdoor advertising, the interactive billboard delivers a much stronger experience than the static poster. Primarily bus stop posters that have video screens and proximity detectors, which let you download ringtone and wallpapers to your mobile phone using Bluetooth.

Newspaper

Newspapers come in different formats for different target consumers, from the trashy to the political. Newspapers have massive circulations and huge consumer impact. Their frequency makes them ideal for time-sensitive advertising opportunities.

Magazine

A fast growing arena with a huge explosion of special interest titles. Advertising and sponsorship opportunities are strong.

Direct Mail

Before the advent of the internet, behaviour-triggered communication was best delivered through direct mail. Now with on-demand digital printing, communication can be completely personalised which is highly effective when well targeted.

Public Relations

A powerful way to reach consumers with press coverage that is highly influential in reaching the desired target audience. Successful PR generates a strong word-of-mouth affect.

Ambient or Guerrilla Marketing

Crazy ideas like hanging washing lines in the street or street graffiti might annoy local authorities but is a powerful way of reaching youth consumers.

Traditional Online Banner

Banner advertising had declining results since its inception but that has steadied now. Standard sizes and formats have made it simple for creative to be run across a number of sites. As agencies discover the potential, newer and more effective concepts are being developed that are substantially better at reaching the consumer. Banners that allow user interaction both aid recall and effectiveness.

Behavioural Rich Media Banner

Advances in banner technology and deliverability have created highly interactive and functional banners that can even allow full shopping within the banner. Behavioural banners are delivered based on specific actions like searching on *holiday* would result in a travel company's banner being displayed.

Organic Search Engine Optimisation

Almost 70% of users start their Internet session at a search engine, which is why achieving top position on the search results is so important. A search engines goal is to deliver the best results for a searched keyword or phrase. By aligning your web site with the search engines goal of delivering the best search information, you can consistently achieve first page rankings in the organic search results.

Pay per Click

These are the paid for text advertisements that are displayed in addition to the organic search results. Companies sponsor specific keywords and bid for consumer clicks. Adverts are positioned based upon how popular they are and how much the advertiser bids for them. They perform very well because they are behaviourally triggered and appear only when someone is searching for specific keywords. Optimisation of the post-click ensures the maximum conversion.

Affiliates

Site partners provide traffic to your site through their own web site and marketing campaign and are paid a percentage of the revenue you make. Very strong returns as you only pay on performance.

Email to Internal List

A great tool for retention marketing is regular email newsletters with promotions and product offers. Segmentation of emails for specific users provides more value to the consumer whilst behavioural emails are proving very effective. An example of behavioural emails is when a consumer fails their ecommerce checkout process and later receives a follow up email.

Email to 3rd Party List

Opt-in email lists can be purchased from third parties, similar to direct mail. Third party email list marketing can take the form of dedicated email newsletters to advertisements from a number of companies on a single newsletter.

SMS

Huge penetration of mobile phone usage makes SMS marketing very powerful. Successful campaigns that are carefully opted in are tremendously effective at reaching the consumer wherever they may be.

RSS

RSS stands for *Really Simple Syndication* and is a basic text file in XML that people can subscribe to through newer browsers and RSS readers as well as use on their Live.com or Google.com portal home pages. The power of RSS is the ability to deliver content in a timely fashion and allow people to use this content in a way that suits them best. For example, a corporate travel agent could subscribe to RSS feeds from major airlines to get the latest offers, travel or destination information updates. It is important that RSS feeds are either available in many different versions or can be customised for the consumers' needs.

Widgets/Gadgets

These little pieces of functionality are added to web pages and computer desktops and provide an innovative marketing opportunity for companies. A blatantly commercial offering is unlikely to be used by consumers but a widget that is useful can generate substantial positive behavioural influence. An example is a widget for TVGuide.co.uk that displays what is currently on TV now – this is both useful to consumers and provides a strong marketing mechanism.

Additional Opportunities to Influence the Customer

Marketing outside standard advertising is now also under the remit of Marketing 2.0. Anything that influences the customer to purchase is now the responsibility of the marketing team and this is much greater than just advertising. With lots of marketing ending up at the next contact point whether that is a web page, telephone assistant or in-store these have to be optimised and each touch point managed to ensure that marketing communication is appropriately translated. It isn't any good if your telesales team isn't aware of your promotion or the web site does not reflect the message that was on your banners. With Marketing 2.0, these elements can no longer be restricted to external departments.

Micro Site

A specialist site that clearly delivers information that is often difficult to do on the main web site. This could be interactive, video based or just text based pages on the Internet. For example, consumers could be helped with new technology advice for something like HD TVs that would include a complete explanation of the benefits of the technology.

Rich Application Interface

With relatively new technology like AJAX, an internet user can get a much richer user experience and is no longer restricted by page-after-page reloads that internet sites are known for. With this technology, users can drag around maps on Google Maps, change a quantity on their basket and have the basket recalculate without a reload. The objective with any rich application implementation is the improvement in usability, which often leads to improved to site conversion. GAP.com is an innovative user of this technology and allow you to view the product size and colour details straight from a catalog page.

Contact Optimisation Systems

Measuring the interactions of every user often requires the implementation and management of Customer Relationship Management (CRM) and Customer Experience Management (CEM) systems. They normally aggregate activity from the call-centre, web site and in-store into a single system to allow the easy and simple management of the customer interface and a much clearer understanding of consumer as a whole enabling a better customer experience.

Viral Campaigns

The internet equivalent of word-of-mouth is the viral campaign. The campaign entertains and provides the ability for people to collaborate and/or win prizes. A successful campaign generates interest to encourage people to forward-to-friends and family and can be anything from a game to an instant win competition.

Online Checkout Optimisation

With Marketing 2.0, optimisation of the checkout process becomes the responsibility of the marketing team. Looking at the steps the customer takes on the web site to the final checkout process, analysing drop-offs and optimising the checkout process can increase site conversion and profitability. Implementing single-page checkout can lead to an increase in checkout conversion of up to 50%.

Call-Centre Optimisation

Every touch point has an impact on the customer including call-centre staff. Optimisation of the call-centre systems, staff training and queuing systems can improve the performance of a call-centre. Newer technologies remove the keypad menus with a simple speech recognition technology that responds to common structured requests. Providing appropriate systems where every call-centre person can see a centralised view of the consumer empowers an operator to deal with every customer request rather than transferring calls between operators and is now what customers expect.

Marketing Channels Table

Marketing Channel	Targeting	Measurement Accuracy	Metrics	A/B Test	Pros	Cons
Traditional TV Commercials	Low -demographic geographic. Behaviour Targeting - No	Low unless direct response	CPM, GRP, TRP	Creative, Time of day, Channel, Geography, Ad Length	Still best for mass consumer reach	Expensive High CPMs Declining Ad recall
On-demand/IPTV Commercials	High – per home. Behaviour Targeting - Yes	Medium – dependant on whether the consumer can transact through the TV/computer	CPM, CPA, CPR	Creative, Time of day, Channel, Geography, Ad Length, Household, Programme	Future for TV delivery	New and relatively unproven
Radio	Low -demographic geographic. Behaviour Targeting - No	Low unless direct response	CPM, GRP, TRP	Creative, Time of day, Channel, Geography, Ad Length	Great for localised advertising & reach the car driver	Little Targeting
Internet Radio	Medium/High – Possible to recognise individual consumers. Behaviour Targeting - Maybe	Low/High – measured through direct response	CPM	Creative, Time of day, Channel Geography, Ad Length, Per Listener	High potential	New, Mostly limited to computers
Podcasts	Medium – Possible to recognise individual consumers but podcast generally created for a group. Behaviour Targeting - No	Low unless direct response	Per cast, CPM	Content, length	Huge take-up and great way of reaching savvy consumer	Likely to listen to entertainment and news. Can forward past advertising
Traditional outdoor	Low – geographic areas – roads/train/subway/ underground, billboard size. Behaviour Targeting - No	Low/Medium	Sheet Size, GRP, TRP	Geography, Creative, Location, Size	Easily recognised, large time spent reading when people are waiting for busses or trains	Not particularly targeted unless running local campaigns and difficult to measure performance

Marketing Channel	Targeting	Measurement Accuracy	Metrics	A/B Test	Pros	Cons
Interactive Outdoor	Medium – Consumers can select what they want. Proximity detectors can activate video when someone is in region. Behaviour Targeting - Yes triggered by interaction or proximity.	Medium – Bluetooth enables measurement and counting of content download.	Per unit, interactions, Bluetooth downloads, proximity detection	Geography, Creative, Location, Size, Interactions	Engages much more than traditional outdoor advertising	Relatively new with lots of experimentation and testing
Newspaper	Medium – geographic, day, section and demographic. Behaviour Targeting - No	Low unless direct response	Ad size, circulation, geography	Ad size/position, maybe geography	Proven and recognised medium. Fast lifecycle	Difficult to measure
Magazine	Medium – geographic, day, section and demographic. Behaviour Targeting - No	Low unless direct response	Ad size, circulation, geography	Ad size/position, maybe geography	Proven and recognised medium good for specialist interest advertising.	Difficult to measure
Direct Mail	Reach and communicate individually to consumers. Behaviour Targeting - Yes	High – ability to measure the response through all channels through vouchers/codes	Number sent, variance, response rate, Undelivered	Content, size, envelope, creative, day, per consumer	Proven, ideal for behavioural	Badly targeted pieces add to consumer annoyance
Public relations	Medium – objective is to get coverage in press, magazines, TV, online where your potential customers are likely to be reading an article. Behaviour Targeting - No	Normally difficult to measure direct relationship	Column inches, Channel, Coverage	Distribution groups	Highly influential if well done	Companies that tend to already have a high profile tend to get more PR

Marketing Channel	Targeting	Measurement Accuracy	Metrics	A/B Test	Pros	Cons
Ambient or Guerrilla marketing	Medium – being creative in reaching people. Behaviour Targeting - Low-High	Low – difficult to determine direct relationship	Activity and impact	Idea	Above the clutter of traditional advertising. Creates word of mouth	Legal issues with placement especially projections. Might not remember the brand and could have negative impact on the brand.
Traditional Online banner	Medium – often done across a network of sites or a single site but can be targeted per consumer. Behaviour Targeting - No	High	CPM, CPA, CPR, Post impression revenue, Interaction	Formats, creative, placement	Creative flexibility, new formats like takeovers	Banner blindness makes people miss ads
Behavioural rich media banner	High – delivered based on specific actions like search keywords or pages. Behaviour Targeting - Yes	High	CPM, CPA, CPR, Post impression revenue, Interaction	Formats, creative, placement	Highly effective	Limited inventory
Organic search engine optimisation	High – help people that need to find your site find it through search engines. Behaviour Targeting - Yes	High – see a change in site traffic from search engines	Site visitors, time on site, funnel steps	Different optimisation techniques inc page urls	Every site needs to visible to search engines	Visibility is often complex to understand & may require specialist advice
Pay per click search	High – Behaviour and contextual based upon keywords that people enter in search engines. Behaviour Targeting - Yes	High – see a change in site traffic and keywords, plus revenue by keywords	Site visitors, time on site, funnel steps	Ad text, included prices, landing pages	Strong ROI. Very targeted.	Declining ROI
Affiliates	High – Partners advertise for you. Behaviour Targeting - Yes	High – based on actual revenue	Sales, EPC	Different creative, commission schemes	Costs directly proportional to sales	Time consuming to cultivate key affiliates

Marketing Channel	Targeting	Measurement Accuracy	Metrics	A/B Test	Pros	Cons
Email to Internal List	High – unique emails can be created for every user. Behaviour Targeting - Yes	High - based on opens, clicks and actual revenue	Click thorughs, Open rates, Sales	subject lines, call to action, main title, body copy, photographs, promotional offer, product price, free shipping	Strong ROI. Best way to communicate to existing customers	Too much email can be regarded as spam. Inbox deliverability
Email to 3rd Party List	Medium – bulk lists are often generated from competition web sites. Behaviour Targeting - Dependant on provider	High - based on opens, clicks and actual revenue	CPC, CPR, CPA Click through, Open rates, Sales	Subject lines, call to action, main title, body copy, photographs, promotional offer, product price, free shipping	Well targeted lists and offers produce good results	look bad for the brand as too many emails could be regarded as spam
SMS	High – unique text messages can be created for every user. Behaviour Targeting - Yes	High – based on reply or web/wap/i-mode interaction	No sent, replies, text ins	Text, dedicated short codes	Strong ROI high SMS usage	Legal restrictions on opt-in data
RSS	Medium – feeds can be uniquely generated but are normally created for groups. Behaviour Targeting - No but could be	High – based on downloads and clicks	Clicks, Subscriptions	Content variation	Bypasses SPAM and deliverability email issues that are problematic in channels like email	Penetration is limited to early adopters at the moment.

GRP – Gross Rating Points

TRP – Targeted Rating Points

CPM – Cost per thousand

CPA – Cost per Acquisition

CPR – Cost per Registration

EPC – Earnings per thousand Clicks

SMS – Short messaging service

RSS – Really Simple Syndication

Marketing Optimisation and Measurement

Multi-Variant Testing

With near real-time measurement on online campaigns it is possible to conduct A/B or multi-variant testing. This is where you run variations of a campaign to test to see which one performs better and then run with the better performing campaign to ensure that you get the best results. This can be continued to ensure that campaigns are optimised on an on-going basis. Just testing one variable at a time (A/B testing) though accurate can be time-consuming so multi-variant testing allows the testing of multiple changes at once to test campaigns much faster. To test a typical email campaign you would try alternative subject lines, calls to action, main body copy, photographs, prices and promotional offers.

Single Measurement Tool for ROI Analysis

Measurement of performance has never been more important. Current marketing model relies on disparate tools where you continuously run the risk of allocating sales against multiple channels and campaigns. With Marketing 2.0, you need a single measurement and analysis tool. Every campaign, creative change, placement variation, copy change will lead to a variation in results. With different measurement metrics for everything from newspapers to site enhancements, it becomes difficult to measure the performance of a medium or campaign against another. The reality is that there are two clear metrics that do not change namely sales and cost. With these metrics, the ROI can be calculated. Additional metrics need to be measured for each channel, like interaction for banners or reach for TV campaigns. These metrics are appropriate for measuring future campaigns against the same medium but more care should be taken when comparing across channel. For example, reach on a TV campaign maybe different to reach from a pay-per-click search campaign, as the search campaign is likely to be targeted by behaviour i.e. someone typed a specific keyword into a search engine to cause the advert to be displayed.

Continual optimisation

One of the key problems with the current marketing practice is that it has not kept up with the change in consumers' behaviour, particularly in the last few years. To counter-act this it is essential that campaigns are measured on an on-going basis and continually optimised to ensure the best marketing mix. The slow take-up of MSN's own pay-per-click search engine showed that early adopters could make substantial returns whilst most advertisers lagged behind.

Behaviour Influence Measurement

In addition to this standard centralised marketing measurement a new metric for measuring the influence a particular piece of marketing has on a consumer has to be created. This *behavioural influence* metric combines a number of data points and consumer surveys to see changes in intent based on particular pieces of marketing. For example, a custom car configurator tool on Porsche's web site would have a very high behavioural influence, which could be determined by surveying consumers pre-usage and post-usage to determine how much more likely they were to buy a car after using the configurator tool. With Marketing 2.0, *behavioural influence* measurement will become the standard.

Optimising Marketing Mix

With so many marketing options available and the need to be consumer centric and behaviour driven, it becomes essential to analyse all the mediums available and make objective judgements on their capabilities rather than focusing on past successes. A successful marketer will maximise their returns by correctly allocating budget across all their media options. Once media spend is allocated it should be constantly optimised to deliver the best return on investment. Allocation of media budget should no longer be revisited on an annual basis but much more fluidly. Constant optimisation and reallocation of budget can lead to substantial improvements in return, for example Ford used XMOS, a media allocation tool by IAB that showed that if they moved just 2% of their advertising spend to online would result in a $90 million greater return.[6]

Predictive Analysis

Looking at past campaign performance it is possible to help predict the performance of future campaigns. A predictive analysis tool will take a comprehensive set of data and look to define the specific variables that are most likely to result in a particular result. This can be used to determine the most important factors at predicting the sale of a particular product from a whole host of data, which includes the customers' demographic and behavioural data. Typical predictive analysis tools are more effective with large amounts of data and will take around 20% of the data to build a statistical model and the rest of the data to validate the model. For instance, providing lots of information about the sales of a particular product like bottled beer might show a strong correlation with time of day and customer gender i.e. men buying beer on the way home from work. Successful marketing companies use these tools to give them much stronger insight into their campaign content as well as predicting with greater accuracy the performance of a particular piece of marketing with some campaigns being able to be predicted to an excess of 80% accuracy.

Marketing 2.0 Additional Considerations

Privacy Concerns

Something that should not be disregarded is the increased level of concern from mass consumers that fear that the huge amount of data that is collected about them could damage people's personal freedom. The reality is that this has probably already happened, for a small amount of money you can easily get significant amounts of data for a person and can build up an accurate profile. However, an organisation should always be ethical at securing customer data and ideally, this data should never be sold or transmitted outside the organisation. As the sophistication of personalisation grows so will the level of consumer understanding.

Agency Selection

Implementation of a Marketing 2.0 model takes many partners, internal and external working together in a collaborative effort. Many companies try to implement a single agency approach to improve efficiency and communication but seeing the varied channels and technical understanding, this rarely proves to be successful. It is not necessarily that agencies are not able to be cross-disciplined, many of the large ones have the capability to buy the smaller niche agencies and the resources to staff up but the culture, expertise and innovation of a specialist cannot be de-valued. Niche agencies have the power to really shape new media and create the thinking that allows the commercialisation of new ideas. The reality is agency co-ordination is expensive so a balanced model is required that minimising the number of agencies whilst choosing specialist agencies that are experts in their area.

5 Key Points for Marketing 2.0

1. Marketing 2.0 is about changing customers' behaviour at key stages throughout their buying process, not media to buy.
2. Ask the question *Would you recommend us to a friend?* Use the results. Share them internally.
3. Behavioural marketing is the low hanging fruit that will deliver great returns for little investment.
4. Create *behaviour influence* metrics when analysing your marketing that look at the marketing elements that have the most influence on your customers' behaviour and intent to purchase.
5. Use a single tool for measurement. You cannot make good decisions without good data. Separate tools from different providers risk double allocation of sales and are at the root of your problems.

Social 2.0

Social 2.0

The web seamlessly integrates text, photos and videos without any regard for distance. This technological infrastructure has become the foundation for global communities of like-minded individuals, that both have the power to change and shape people's thinking. This community has a huge authority. They influence corporations, governments and each other to achieve results that no individual could match. Harnessing the power of the community is the key to gaining real advantage in the ecommerce landscape. Once this community spirit is harnessed it becomes a strong barrier for competitors Sure you can set-up another site selling books but how are you going to get all the user-generated book reviews and lists that give real power to the Amazon purchasing experience.

Many companies are worried that this community power removes their influence and in some ways, it does but companies that fail to embrace social networks will be the ones that have most to lose in the future. Part of the corporate responsibility is in creating the tools that the community need to make the most out of social networking, the other part is removing obstacles and embracing this new paradigm. The value in delivering social elements is more than just anecdotal, social elements deliver:

- Product innovation through suggestions and feedback
- Product descriptions beyond the manufacturer's, targeted by consumers for consumers. E.g., *how easy is it to increase hard disk space in this PVR myself?*
- Product evaluations through reviews and ratings
- Peer customer support and advice
- Customer advocates
- Knowledge from information

The greatest power will come from companies that leave the product delivery to the consumers. Imagine creating a toolset and letting your community create the product. That is exactly what is happening at the moment with:

- **Opensource,** which provides a community to build and enhance an application.
- **Web services,** which allow the community to decide how they use and integrate your application and data.
- **Mash-ups**, which join disparate web services to provide innovative and novel functionality.

In this chapter, we look at *how user generated content drives online community, why the community is valuable* and *how you can harness social elements* to help push forward the next generation of ecommerce.

Why Is The Community So Powerful?

Humans are a social species. We rely on trusted networks of people that help us make decisions. Before the internet these networks were restricted to people we knew directly in the real world from doctors to friends. Now, the whole internet community is a potential advisor. Have you noticed the validation that many people need for making a purchasing decision? You have probably heard these questions in conversations - *Do you think this looks good on me? Do you think I should spend that much on a pair of shoes? What plasma/laptop should I get?* Everyone wants reassurance that they are making the right choice and are getting the best deal. There are varying levels of trust in an advisory relationship from the surgeon that we have to trust implicitly to the sales assistant that we hope is giving you the best advice. In all these relationships, you hope that the person giving you the advice is unbiased, honest and does not have any conflicts of interest that could influence the advice they give you, like extra commissions on a particular product. However, when was the last time a shop assistant recommended a product that they did not stock? Online communities resolve a number of the issues regarding single or small groups of advisors because of the online community size and specialisation. This size ensures that errors and biased information should be picked up quickly, and again because of the size there is a greater likelihood of someone sharing the exact same issues as you. In addition, even though the majority of people may not be active members of a community, they do rely on communities of specialists when it comes to making their purchasing decisions from finance to electronics.

The Power of the Influencer

Some people have considerably more influence than others do on you. For example, your best friend has more of an influence than say someone you just met on the street. There are some people, which by their position in society influence more people than the average person. These people are called influencers and you might imagine they are the leaders of our society but more often than not, they are Celebes! However hard someone tries to avoid it, these influencers affect our decision-making processes. Some ecommerce sites like Amazon have been early in understanding this by allowing many community features like reviews and specialist lists. Influencers add the most value to the social network, are often the strongest advocates and the most important when trying to harness the power of the community.

The Value of a Social Network

A network has a value proportional to the square of the number of people within that network. This is easily illustrated through the counting of connections between the network members. A network with two members has only one connection. A network with four members has six connections and is therefore 6 times more valuable. Taking a network with 1,000 members would show 1,000,000 connections. Network economics shows why auction sites and community sites that have the greatest contributing members have the greatest value and tend to be the most successful. Even if a competitor manages to get half the number of members, they would only have a quarter of the value and this would show up in the reduced amount of content or liquidity on the site.

The value of the Network

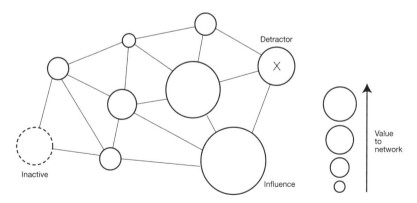

The Principles of Social Networking

Four main elements form the ability to create a social network online.

1. **The primary content** that the social element references. This could be any piece of content on your site like a product, user, photograph, video, content or brand.

2. **The social tools** (All of the social elements can consist of video, photos, audio and text):
   a. Forums – Single/Multi-threaded, FAQs, Comments
   b. Reviews
   c. Blogs
   d. Wikis
   e. Tags
   f. Lists
   g. Behaviour based social elements like *Customers who bought this product also bought...*, *if you rated this item highly you may also like* or *93% of people feel these items match.*

3. **The feedback mechanism**, which could be any of the social elements themselves but tends to be a rating.

4. **The changes to the social elements over time** i.e. the rate that they are updated or the changes in rating scores over time all go towards showing changing attitudes towards specific social content. For instance, a product that initially had a very high rating may see its rating decline over time as newer products appear on the market and this could easily be illustrated by a graph.

With today's technology these social elements do not have to be restricted to one ecommerce site and can now be shared across a number of sites to take advantage of a much larger network and therefore a greater value. For example, a review of a digital camera on a shopping site would consist of reviews from everyone who bought that camera on that site and many other sites, providing a much more valuable experience for the consumer. This shared review and shared forums technology is providing the key functionality for a number of new start-up companies that are embracing social networking for enhanced customer experiences.

In the upcoming sections, we will explain the primary content, the social tools, feedback mechanisms and the changes to social tools over time. In addition, we will look at facilitating social technologies through opensource community development, web services and mash-ups.

1. The Referenced Primary Content

This primary content is the element that the social tools like forums, blogs, and comments reference. This primary element could be a TV show on an entertainment site, product on an ecommerce site or a user on a community site. The strength of the social model is that the primary content can be anything from words, pictures and video. For example, a primary content of a photograph could have forums, reviews, ratings, blogs, wikis, lists and comments about it. In addition, because it is a photo these elements could be placed on different parts of the photograph. A site can have many different primary content elements and have any number of different social tools attached to them. This is clearly seen on Amazon where a particular product has *reviews, ratings, forums, wikis, lists* and *customers who bought this product also bought* all on a single product page.

2. The Social Tools

There are a number of different types of social element that vary by the content they store and their structure. These main social elements are commonly known as forums, wikis, blogs, reviews, tags and lists. Popular social sites like myspace.com and linkedin.com are combinations of these social elements.

a. Forums

Discussion forums are used to store conversations between people and are often used for question and answers elements. Each reply to a forum is called a thread and forums can be in single threaded or multi-threaded. With a single thread, entries are normally displayed under each other based on time of entry while a multi-threaded forum is more complex and allows people to create a thread based on any previous forum entry rather than just relying on date. Multi-threaded forums are typically displayed in a hierachical tree view and are ideal for dealing with complex discussions and taking topics off at a tangent without destroying the original thread. Multi-threaded forums are powerful tools but do provide a little complexity to the average Internet user. Single threaded forums are also named as FAQs, Feedback and Comments sections and provide a simple and easy why to create social content. Users love to talk about things they are passionate about and forums provide an easy method for doing this.

b. Reviews

Allowing a consumer to rate and review items generates considerable amount of value to the network of consumers. Many reviews are well written and clearly demonstrate both the positive and negative points for a particular product, service or brand, Additions of both photographs and the recent popularity of video reviews delivers even greater value to the consumer network. For example, looking at a piece of furniture photographed in someone's room gives a clear idea of scale layout and possible uses. Reviews and in-room photographs could be created by the site itself but the unbiased nature of customer reviews and the consumer perspective is something that is not easily replicated. Reviews also have the advantage of showing that someone else has bought the product, which can be a great motivator for people considering a purchase. Many sites are concerned about the risks of including reviews, especially if they are negative, but research has found that most reviews are positive and that negative reviews provide a feedback mechanism for the site and manufacturers that lets them refine and develop a product.

c. Blog

Blogs are online diaries and have taken the internet by storm. Blogs enable the consumer to be an online voice and easily publish their own ideas, views and opinions. Great blog sites are visited by millions of people and often provide an insight and specialism that the traditional media has either ignored or not been viable to reach. Magazines and newspapers are driven by circulation and advertisers while blog writers have none of those restrictions. Where a magazine or newspaper may have provided a review of the latest mobile phone that consisted of a photograph and a page of copy, a blog will provide pages of detailed information with photographs and video of everything from unpacking the box, inserting the batteries, plugging in connectors and the phone interface. For the serious purchaser, this gives an insight that was never possible before and is fabulous if you are going to spend a month's salary on an expensive technology purchase like a plasma screen.

d. Wikis

A wiki allows collaborative and easy creation of content. Any user can go in and create content as well as amend existing content. This collaborative content creation is an ideal way of getting a community of knowledgeable people to agree, share and document their thinking. There is a version control system within a wiki that allows the rolling back to previous content that has been submitted erroneously. One of the strongest validations of the Wiki is Wikipedia, which provides an online encyclopaedia to rival the best offline equivalents.

Wiki technology is perfect for consumers to create their own detailed product information. Typically, ecommerce web sites take information created by the manufacturer, with a product wiki consumers can create product information that is written by a consumer for other consumers. Wikis are perfect for items where the consumer's knowledge of the product can often outweigh the manufacturer's, for instance consumers would include whether a particular DVD player is multi region or whether the hard disk can be replaced for a larger one. Amazon was one of the first companies to include wikis on their product pages.

e. Tags

Tags allow consumers to mark a product with their own words just like a post-it note but electronically. A consumer can add their own tags to a product or any social element for future reference and recall. These tags can be held privately for that consumer or be shared with the general consumer base as a clear way of categorising and finding products. For example, a consumer could tag up their favourite CDs so they do not have to remember whether they had heard the music before and what their opinion was.

f. Lists

Lists are about users generating their own collection of items that can be shared with people. These could be lists of favourite TV programmes, music, bookmarks, products, videos, photos practically anything including lists of lists. When an item that you like is on a list, the odds are that the other items on the list are likely to be of interest. In addition, if you find another consumer that has similar profile to you it is likely that their lists will be of interest to you.

A specific type of list for ecommerce sites is a wish List. If you have ever received something useless for a gift, you will love the concept of wish lists. A wish list is a set of products that you would like for a gift for an event in your life. These events could range from Birthdays, Weddings, Anniversaries, Births, and Christmas. The list contains your favourite items and additional attributes that include personal comments and a level of priority. These lists can be searched by friends and family to find the perfect gift for you, for any occasion. Ecommerce 2.0 sites are also adding the ability for you to upload video and photos to go with your list, so for example you could give a personal video message to all your guests for your wedding gift list.

g. Behaviour Based Social Elements

Not every social element has to consist of a consumer writing, uploading pictures/video or clicking a rating, their actions can be used to derive social elements. The concept is to look for patterns based on consumers behaviour whether that is a purchase, a rating, a click, time spent watching a video, amount of submitted forum entries, etc. Any action that a consumer makes can be recorded and then related to other actions to create a pattern. An example of this is the *customers who bought this product also bought these products* functionality, which looks at the purchase behaviour of customers. This can be expanded to other behaviours, like *customers who rated this TV show highly also rated these shows highly* to show other TV shows that you may like. New sites like 6pm.com are allowing customers to rate how good a pair of shoes and handbag look together, so other customers can always get the best match.

Customers Who Bought This Product, Also Bought…

A great piece of technology that many ecommerce sites have now looks at all previous orders from all customers to see what else they bought with that particular product. These are ranked on the theory that if people bought many of these items together then they must be good together. For music, this gives a strong insight into bands that you may be interested in, based on the band you like. *Customers who bought* functionality also has the secondary affect of showing that other people have bought this item before giving consumers the confidence to make a purchase.

3. Feedback Mechanisms

Ratings

Ratings can be one of the social elements and form the most popular feedback mechanism for social elements like forums, reviews and lists. There are two elements in generating ratings, one is identifying whether an overall rating or detailed attributes like quality and value should be rated. Secondly, a rating can consist of stars, a score or percentage. A star system is useful for consumer web sites as it is easy to understand, the downside is that it is difficult to see the differences in ratings where many items have close scores and a lot of items end up with five stars. A popular rating system for customer reviews is the *Yes/No* question *Was this review useful?* and is used to position the best reviews. Ratings should be ranked using a Bayesian weighting formulae that looks at the number of votes and the average rating to ensure that items with one score of 10 does not out rank an item that has 100 votes and an average rating of 9.5.

4. Changes over Time

Looking at the changes in the social elements and the ratings over time can show some interesting insight into the changes in importance of certain content. If for instance, a TV show that used to get high ratings and suddenly starts to receive a large number of low ratings, would indicate that show could be going out of favour with consumers. This could be expanded to a complete genre. Similarly, this could be applied to a particular product or manufacturer. This kind of data provides strong consumer insight. The sites that have this information at their disposal are in a stronger position to feed this back to the source and actually change the structure and mix of their offering.

Opensource – the Community Way

Opensource is an interesting community development model, which is driving many software projects forward. It consists of a community of developers working together to develop specific functionality into an application. This movement is powerful because it engages a huge community of programmers to deliver something towards a common goal mostly with no financial reward. Some members of the community are developing features for themselves and then these are shared back into the collective project. Proponents argue that this is the future of application development. The power of this community is something that may have some strong potential in the ecommerce marketplace, not just through community developed ecommerce platforms but more profoundly through community driven retail where whole groups of people are working together to deliver and run an ecommerce offering. They assimilate the customers and the retailer creating strategic direction, product mix and services through a group.

Web services and Mash-ups

Web services are powerful because they allow a community of developers to use functionality and data from your web site in their own particular way. They can integrate it and use it in various different ways from simply presenting your products or content in a different way to more complicated incarnations where they aggregate your data with other providers to create their own ecommerce stores. The power of web services comes when disparate providers are combined in what is called mash-ups to provide functionality that is both useful and in some cases revolutionary. Most people are using web services from Amazon, Ebay, Google and Live.com to create novel functions, like HousingMaps.com, which takes classified rental properties from Craigslist.com and displays them on a Google map so users can easily find houses to rent near them. Ecommerce sites should embrace this open movement by providing their own web services.

5 Key Points for Social 2.0

1. Embrace consumers and let them tell you what they want.
2. Make it easy for them to feedback to you by providing the social tools from forums to reviews.
3. Incorporate these social elements into your whole organisation from product development to site enhancements.
4. Mix feedback with behavioural measures to provide strong social elements.
5. Monitor and report changes over time to visualise changes in consumer behaviour.

Engage 2.0

Engage 2.0

Many pages in this book are guiding you into becoming a customer centric organisation, placing the customer in the centre of everything you do. With Engage 2.0, this chapter will discuss concepts that will take that customer centric approach and use it to build a long lasting, loyal customer relationship. Engage 2.0 is about evolving the customer experience. It is about providing the right tools to help customers make a better purchasing decision. Engage 2.0 is about building a relationship that both the customer and the retailer can thrive on.

In this chapter, we will cover a number of different tool sets that can be used to improve your overall customer relationship, namely:

- Loyalty programmes.
- Providing functionality to let your customers become brand advocates and recommend your company to others.
- Helping customers find the right products for themselves and in turn increasing sales and reducing returns.
- Providing a better shopping experience on your site.
- Considering your social responsibility as an organisation.
- Looking at new technologies that provide better interfaces to improve the customer experience.
- How to measure your reputation and the experience you offer?

Engage 2.0 is about understanding the consumers needs and using technology available to meet those needs. The web has evolved considerably over the years and yet, however great they may be, the offerings provided by companies such as Amazon, EBay and Google have not changed that dramatically. This may have something to do with the technology and the time to market new solutions or it may be that Web 2.0 is not about big step changes but about making baby steps and evolving your offering slowly over time.

Loyalty 2.0

Many consumers are looking for a company to do business with repeatedly. A company they like. A company that looks after them. A company they can trust and respect. If a retailer can deliver on these promises, they will have gained a loyal consumer. For a retailer to gain this loyalty they need to offer a compelling experience that is inline or exceeding the customer's expectation. Loyal customers will trust your recommendations and become your greatest advocates, referring additional customers from friends and family. In Ecommerce 2.0, consumers have the power to build and destroy companies. Having a company culture that fosters loyalty and actively monitors experience to make sure it is in line with the brand values is now the key.

Many loyalty schemes today are focused on incentivising the consumer in return for points, in simple terms offering a small bribe to encourage the consumer to return. This points collecting customer is not necessarily the same as a loyal consumer. For instance, someone who regularly collects points may just be a well-informed consumer collecting points from multiple companies whilst there may be many consumers who are loyal to an organisation but just have not got around to collecting points. Using third party points or rewards based loyalty programmes can help build loyal consumers but the loyalty is attached to the rewards scheme rather than the organisation and presents a number of risks to the retailer, especially if they were to depart the scheme. This was seen with Barclaycard leaving the Nectar loyalty programme to be quickly replaced by American Express, leaving thousands of Nectar points collecting Barclaycard consumers being motivated to switch credit card providers to continue collecting points. Also, rewards based loyalty schemes work well with necessity driven repeat purchases such as Business flights, Grocery shopping, Health and beauty products but not as well with big ticket occasional purchases such as cars or items with a high emotional attachment such as shoes or jewellery.

Very few retailers have systems or processes in place to allow them to develop and foster long-term relationships with their consumers and a common misunderstanding is that a loyalty scheme is merely about launching a point-based system. Loyalty 2.0 is more than just points or rewards; it is about developing a holistic view of loyalty and looking at what behaviour triggers loyalty. Analysis of customers throughout their buying process and analysis of changing behaviour through marketing campaigns can help deliver a strong loyalty-marketing programme. This loyalty programme can consist of rewards, points or special promotions, which can be communicated via email, online or direct mail to an existing customer. Every communication should be tailored and personal and should take into account:

1. **The reward** – Loyalty rewards need to go further than just rewarding a customer for placing an order, rewards should extend to providing points for opening an email, writing a review or simply returning to the site.

2. **The experience** – Providing a great experience is key to building a loyal customer, this involves easy processes and tailoring each experience for the customer, whether they are re-visiting your site or calling to chase an order.

3. **The brand** – Creating a brand a customer can offer lifetime loyalty too is difficult, especially with products that are

targeted at a particular age group, or demographic such as mother with young children (eventually the children grow up). With loyalty 2.0, the brand can evolve a new strategy as their consumers develop through their lifecycle.

As Harry Potter ages so does the reader

 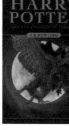  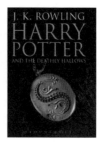

Ages 10-12   Ages 12-14   Ages 14-16   Ages 18+

A Loyalty 2.0 program should engage the customer from the initial contact, providing a great experience from the outset, first impressions count. New systems need to be implemented to reward the consumer for their loyalty, with more that just points but with a better experience. With this combination of systems and processes, retailers should be in a strong position to build a valuable business from their loyal customer base.

Word Of Mouth 2.0

A customer wants to shout about a great experience or a great discovery. It is human nature. The incentive is the respect gained from peers for the discovery. A customer will also trade in respect for other incentives such as hard cash. In his book, 'The Tipping Point', Malcolm Gladwell explains that the rapid spread of news through a community via word of mouth is largely driven by the actions of a few well-informed and connected individuals. However in a recent study conducted by Duncan J Watts of the Columbia university, research shows that *'the widespread propagation of influence through networks - is delivered in the presence not of a few influential's but, rather, of a critical mass of easily influenced people'*. It is the later theory that indicates that targeting ordinary users and providing them with social networking tools to recommend your product or service will help organisations reach a mass audience. Rather than simply providing a link to recommend your product to a single friend, they need to be provided the tools to recommend your product to a mass of consumers.

The majority of ecommerce sites now provide the ability to let customers recommend a product to a friend, the *tell-a-friend* link is usually next to every product or displayed as the *forward-to-friend* button on an email. Looking at the analytics figures these links only have a click through rate of 0.2% [An average figure taken from analytics from 100 UK sites, Rank Me Report 2007], an extremely low figure that does not fully justify the presence of such links. Traditional *tell-a-friend* links are used to capitalise on the one-to-one relationships the customers have with their friends and family. In the customer's eyes this tool is not enough, they would rather send the URL directly to the relevant person. Retailers need to use this space to capitalise on the one-to-many relationships, one or more degrees of separation away that customers have with everyone they know. It is unlikely they want to send an email to everyone they know but there are other platforms available to allow them to broadcast the benefits of your products.

Word-of-Mouth 2.0 is about providing such tools. Functionality that allows customers to recommend your organisation and your products to everyone they know on their social network. To facilitate these activities, retailers need to look at the following:

1. **Add social tools to your site**. Wikis, blogs, forums, reviews and ratings all add social elements to a site that lets you leverage a word-of-mouth marketing. The social network will give the acknowledgement/respect to the users who provide realistic, easily digested feedback. Further details of social networking are covered in the Social 2.0 chapter.

2. **Provide micro-content such as footers, designs, MySpace Widgets or RSS feeds**. These are snippets of information about your brand that users can place on their social space. These messages can then be viewed by others visiting the social spaces. It is important to remember that consumers will not market your offering for nothing, so this content needs to provide a consumer with a valid benefit for recommending your product.

3. **Create your own space on a large social networking site**, such as MySpace, allow people to interact with your brand on this space, this is much easier if the brand in question is targeted to the audience in the chosen social network.

Retailers can look at adding an extra dimension to the Word-of-mouth concept by creating a personal-affiliate program, which consumers can sign up to, Consumers in this program are rewarded for being advocates of your site, and if they drive converting traffic to your site, you will provide them with a commission on the sale.

Cross-Selling/Up-Selling 2.0

The concept of cross-selling/up-selling is common in offline retail stores. When a customer is looking for a tin of beans, they are usually made aware of the organic variety that sits next to their usual purchase. In the online space cross-selling was introduced by Amazon, they launched a more advanced system with *customers who bought also bought*, allowing them to cross sell items that are relevant to the user but not necessarily in the same category. Since then a number of different types of cross-sell and up selling have emerged including:

- **Recommended products** – This is typically a manual recommendation by the retailer.
- **Other items in the same category** – A simply query that returns items within the same category.
- **Picks on the basket page** – The algorithm used here shows products that you most likely to buy based on current items in your basket.
- **Customers who bought this product also bought…** – An algorithm that looks at previous customer purchases to illustrate what people are more likely to buy together.
- **Customers who viewed this product also viewed…** – Looks at the most popular product pages viewed together.
- **Looks good with…** – Showing other items, which may match the product you are viewing by colour, size etc.
- **Quick adds (accessories/extended warranties)** – Items that are needed or typically bought with the purchased product such as batteries or warranties.
- **Complete the look** – A complete selection of products that could be bought together typically a clothing outfit including shoes and matching accessories.

- **Visual match** – Using a visual algorithm to match products pictures with other pictures by shape, size, texture and colour. This can be seen in action at Like.com.
- **Similar by price** – Items that are in a similar price range.
- **Similar by attribute** – Products that match by a particular attribute i.e. on a 5 megapixel digital camera other 5 megapixel cameras will appear, with the ability to search for other products by any other matching attributes.
- **Bundles** – Showing groups of products that can be bought together at a discounted price. For example, a *3 for 2* offer on all vitamins.
- **What do customers buy after viewing this item** – Illustrates what percentage of people bought this product and other products once they ended up on the product page. This illustrates to the site browser what the conversion rate for the product is.
- **Lists this item belongs to** – Shows other items that users have put together with this item through their customised lists.
- **Recently viewed items** – This shows the products that were viewed before the current product.
- **Recommendations based on purchase history** – Shows products that are related based upon the items you bought on previous visits e.g. an album by your favourite music artist.
- **Tag match** – Tags allow a consumer to create their own form of categorisation based on keywords. Products with matching tags are displayed.
- **Customer rated matches** – Items that match based on customer feedback e.g. 6pm.com where shoe and handbag combinations are rated by customers. This actually makes the

cross-selling part of the customer experience.

- **Behaviour based matches** – Showing customers products based on their behaviour and contextual relationships between products. A great example of this is when a user is browsing through travel guides about Florida, then they switch to Art Deco, the customer behaviour has provided some insight and could show architectural books about Miami. In this case, instead of showing related items based on the product being viewed we are showing related items based on customer behaviour.

Initially, the primary reason for implementing such technologies was so that retailers could increase their Average Order Values (AOV) but with Cross-sell/Up-sell 2.0 focus has shifted to providing a better customer experience. An important note is that successful cross selling is not about pushing items that do not sell well or selling items of higher profit, such activities are better performed by home page merchandising or email marketing.

Personalisation 2.0

The evolution of personalisation uses the full set of customer behavioural data to deliver a wonderful customer experience. When a customer visits a site for the first time, they are anonymous, and expecting to be treated as such. As soon as this customer has started their browsing through a site, they have started to provide valuable data on what they are looking for and the type of products they prefer. A typical customer journey may involve:

1. Visit the home page (via search engine)
2. Click on offer on the home page
3. At the product page zoom into a few product images
4. Add the item to the basket

5. Continue shopping by using the search box, entering 'items on sale'
6. View the results, and sort them by brand
7. Leave the site (because they were interrupted by a Skype call.)

In the above site journey, the customer has not divulged any information about himself or herself but analysing the data, retailers can know what the customer is looking for and how they arrived at the site. It is this information that should be used to personalise the experience for the customer. The site should act as a virtual sales assistant and guide the user through their journey, rather than a retail store where the customer is left on their own to find products. Using the same example above, a personalised journey would involve:

1. **Visit the home page (via search engine)** - At this stage you know the search term they have entered in to Google, use this data to show the customer relevant information to the keyword and validate if the landing page is the best choice for that particular keyword. You cannot rely on Google to always link to the correct pages for particular keywords.
2. **Clicked on an offer on the home page** - At this stage, you know the customer can be influenced by the right offer (if it is relevant). When leaving this page, ask them for their email address to send them more offers that are relevant.
3. **Use of product zoom** - The customer is interested in detail. Increase the size of the image as they browse through other product pages.
4. **Using the search box to find, items on sale** - The customer seems like a bargain hunter, so related items and cross-sell items should show items on sale.
5. **Skype call ends their session.**

The journey should be tailored to the consumer. Ecommerce is no longer about simple basket functionality but a more useful, engaging experience. Consumers are impatient and have a high expectancy on the level of functionality provided to them. In order to create a better experience for them, sites should make the purchasing process more intuitive and use the data the customer provides to give them what they want. While the majority of ecommerce sites are designed for a particular demographic or persona, this design is valid for new customers/first time visitors but each customer is different, and returning customers have provided so much additional information their experience can be further customised. Typically, the level of personalisation currently available is usually limited to products and offers, but should look at personalising the experience for each consumer, and evolving this experience over time. Amazon use these personalisation techniques to create a customised page under a 'Paul's Amazon.com' tab for a particular consumer but personalisation 2.0 is about delivering a wonderful customer experience throughout the shopping process rather than just highlighting products on a tab. An example would be a travel site that knows enough about their customer to create a perfect itinerary including flights, hotels and entertainment for their week long annual holiday, all with photos, dates and prices – ready to book. Changing elements of the site based on customer behaviour will make the user feel as though they are speaking to a real travel agent and will close the gap between mass delivery and a personal dialogue.

Personalisation 2.0 is about building these great experiences from the first encounter with the customer and making minor adjustments to improve the experience over time. New technology allows retailers the ability to capture the right data over time and make improvements based on this data to build a solution that makes the customer feel comfortable, which engages the customer in to a dialogue with the site and ultimately lead to an improved site conversion rate.

User Innovation 2.0

Opening up your site, via a web service, allows the few technically well informed customers the ability to create improvements in your offering and open up new markets for you. These select few want to be able to evolve the site, moving in a direction the retailer has yet to consider. A web service exposes a sites product information and functionality for usage by other computers, which use this as a foundation to provide improved functionality and improved interfaces. Large retailers such as Amazon, with Amazon Web services, and EBay, with their developer program, have seen as much as 15% of their revenues coming from solutions built by developers in their programmes. For smaller retailers creating an open architecture can involve a lot of work and they are not geared up to provide developer programs, so how can they involve the user to create additional revenue for them. They can start by including users in the development process, a structure that involves the whole user community to provide continuous feedback on existing features and future developments. Customers, who are loyal to the brand and enjoy the experience you offer, want to be involved, they want the ability to send feedback or make suggestions to retailers. They want to be included in beta programmes.

Every site has a customer service email, and usually a feedback form. Many sites also have reviews but all these feedback mechanisms are limited to customer service or feedback on the actual products, rather than the site and the company. Very few sites provide the user the ability to provide feedback on the design of a page, the functionality offered on a site and the overall product range available. Even a simple form asking for candid feedback about the site is difficult to find on ecommerce sites. Just by putting a link to a feedback form and encouraging feedback, sites can generate hundreds of insightful reviews and that help shape the future direction of the organisation.

User Innovation 2.0 is about placing the control of your site into the hands of the consumers, innovation created by organisations is usually need driven, with User Innovation 2.0 retailers can move to creating a demand driven innovation cycle. Customers are now at the forefront, they are interacting with a huge number of online brands and are using thousands of different sites and with this are exposed to huge variety of functionality. Companies should use this experience to drive the future direction of their business. Allow the users to provide feedback and guide the design of your site, select your product range and introduce new functionality. Retailers can either allow them to build this themselves by creating Web services which may allow a user to introduce an offering on a new channel, such as Mobile, alternatively retailers can involve their users in an active ever evolving feedback loop, rather than A/B testing, or user testing conducted by the retailer. Let the user suggest ideas, and let them create their own homepages. Quick wins such as allowing the user to preview an idea and provide feedback, can help filter out unwanted functionality. The UK TV Listings site TVGuide.co.uk has evolved almost completely on consumer feedback, with ideas being stored and added to the development lifecycle. This close alignment with site users has helped it achieve ten times growth in users and traffic in one year, with new functionality added at users request and unused functionality removed.

Ecommerce Search 2.0

58% of customers will use site search to start their ecommerce shopping experience, and users that use the search box are three times more likely to convert. [Gartner, Search Technology Review] If this is the case, then it is strange to consider that the majority of sites use a small text box. Apparently, most ecommerce sites do not have much faith in their search results! Rarely, is the search box a prominent feature on the homepage. Search functionality currently available includes:

1. Site wide product search - usually keywords based.
2. Take into account misspellings and synonyms i.e. *red nail varnish* would also find *crimson nail polish.*
3. Additional sorting based on price, brand, A-Z etc.
4. The ability to filter the search by the attributes returning from the search, like size and colour.
5. Using 'Tags' to navigate through the site.
6. Product comparison.
7. Merchandising within the search results.
8. Visual search by size, shape, colour and texture e.g. Like. com.

There is no doubt that search has improved over the years, but it has yet to evolve to create a compelling user experience, one that replicates and improves on the best in-store experience with knowledgable and helpful staff. Comparison of the in-store and online experience can give insight into the customer's expected experience.

Step 1
In-store experience: Walk into a store and ask the customer service team

for a 6 piece silver cutlery set between £80-£100, with a gothic design.
Online experience should be: Enter '6 Piece silver Cutlery Set, between £80-£100, Gothic design' in the search box.

Step 2

In-store experience: The counter staff or sales assistants would then direct them to the correct aisle where all sets are on display, the customer can then ask any set of questions to narrow down their selection.

Online experience should be: They would then want to be shown all results in relevance order, the site should also allow the user to alter the relevance e.g. Switch from keyword relevance, to A-Z or highest priced first. The search tool should also provide the user with the ability to use a guided navigation system, using different facets of the product. In this example, it would be material, brand, price range etc.

Step 3

In-store experience: The customer has narrowed down their selection to 2-3 items. They ask the sales assistant the main differences between the items they have selected.

Online experience should be: The user can compare items in the results by selecting the items they wish to compare and viewing the products side by side, allowing them to contrast the different features of the product.

Step 4

In-store experience: The customer has selected the item and they are ready to make a buying decision but at any stage, they can change their mind.

Online experience should be: At the stage when they have decided on a product they can click to view all the information but have the ability within the product page to alter their search criteria to continue their search where they left off.

With all the advances in search technology in recent years, there has been little change in the relevance and speed of results. Google is currently the most popular search engine on the planet and offers a simple search, which shows relevant results by the keywords the user has entered. Google is able to deliver relevant results by looking at a number of different elements including content on the page, links from other sites and the context of the links. It is clear that the content on a page is just one of the factors in search, and with Ecommerce Search 2.0, a similar strategy of using additional attributes to build the search results should be used. Additional elements to add into the search algorithm are:

1. Product sales
2. User click history
3. Conversion rates on products
4. Data from product tags
5. Review and forum entries
6. Ratings
7. Returns rates
8. Merchandising – Human guided

For example, a customer who searched '9ct ring' in a jewellery site, and then clicked on the second item on the second page, should cause this product should appear higher up the list when subsequent users visit the site to and search for the same term.

With Ecommerce Search 2.0, companies need to continue to invest in filtered and multi-faceted navigation tools to allow users to drill down through search results by attribute but they also need to look at improving the initial results. Rather than making search more complicated, we need to align our thinking with the user and make it simpler to use. Faceted navigation is still a valuable form of navigation and is especially useful when users are searching for electronic items, but ultimately we need to improve our methods in delivering accurate results using keyword searching.

Ethical & Green 2.0

Consumers are becoming more socially responsible and they want to be associated with companies that have the same thinking. The internet with its vast communications capability fosters a society that can be selective and choose to deal with organisations that are honest, ethical and socially responsible. The sudden and sharp fall in the companies that are trying to deceive the consumer or trading in items which are non-ethical, is due to the internet and the socially aware consumer.

Many organisations are moving to provide a more ethical service, providing better information to the consumer and becoming more open about their offering. Organisation that operate in the following areas, either are in a declining industry or have closed down already:

- Product sales that involve items that are trying to deceive the consumer either directly or through false promises - retailers operating in this sector are disappearing. Examples are photographs that make an item look bigger than they are.
- Products that promise medical cures but are non-medical food supplements or creams e.g. Weight loss pills, hair loss creams, etc.

- Trading in items that are bought to the consumer whilst causing harm to animal or another human, products such as items from low-wage countries where the staff are paid an unfair amount or items that have caused unnecessary harm to animals in the production process. Examples are diamonds and gold from African mines.
- Companies operating in a way that causes a high impact to the environment (social and environment). Oil and Gas companies are particularly susceptible to criticisms.

Any organisation that trades in a responsible way is currently benefiting from better exposure via the media, greater loyalty from the consumer and higher profits as the consumer is usually willing to pay a premium to trade with responsible companies

Ethical & Green 2.0 is about every company becoming aware of their responsibilities. These issues are becoming more and more important. What can business do, here are some concepts for internet retailers:

1. Increase your product range, to include items that are either fair trade, organic or environmentally friendly.
2. Be open and honest about the products you are selling. Do not deceive the consumer in anyway. If a product is new and untested, state that.
3. Provide consumers the ability to book deliveries to reduce their carbon footprint.
4. Allow consumers to reserve online and pickup in-store.
5. Have an ethical packaging policy. Do items really need internal and external packaging?
6. Have a good internal staffing policy. Look at the example of

Innocent drinks, the smoothie company, where employees choose to work because of its strong green and ethical credentials.

7. Create and display your environmental policy online.
8. Be carbon neutral by minimising environmental impact and replacing carbon emissions from transportation and travel, with tree planting.

These issues and many more are becoming imperative in the online world. Now with mass consumer publishing and a strong media stance, organisations should consider the impact to the bottom line of not becoming more green.

Some readers may be thinking if this section should exist in a book about Ecommerce 2.0, but we are in a world where strategy is about more than just about the products you sell, it encompasses everything, including social and environmental issues. Make this an important factor in your business. Even big businesses can fall dramatically when exposed by the media, so never knowingly do wrong.

Rich Application Interface

Any functionality that will improve the customer's online experience will be well received. However, customers do not like the use of rich interfaces if they make an existing process clunkier or if the experience is sidelined in favour of the design. There is no doubt that there will be a few early adopters who like to experience new ways of interacting with your site regardless of the extra effort required but this group will always be the minority. The customer is just looking for a rich experience and this does not necessarily need to be provided using a rich application.

Many retailers have started to implement Rich Application Interfaces (RAI) to allow customers to get a multi-dimensional view of products, zooming in and rotating items to get a real feel of the product. There are also a number of retailers who have started to implement RAI where it can improve the customer experience. RAI provide interactive customer experience and allow the web browser to interchange data with the server without having to re-load the page.

With Ecommerce 2.0, retailers need to move to creating a strategy that caters for novice internet users, as well as a strategy to invest in developing their 2.0 offering. A balanced approach is needed to:

1. Providing a site that functions well for novice internet users, users who may have a slow connection and do not have the bandwidth capability to cope with download intensive sites. In addition, the users who are not used to complex processes or use limited devices like mobile phones.

2. The growing number of web savvy users who are on fast internet connections and seek out better and faster ways to do business with their chosen retailers.

This may sound as if the retailer needs to build an individual site for each type of user, but retailers need to implement a solution that caters for both types of user.

The primary technologies for RAI are:

1. **Flash** – a plugin for the browser provided by Adobe that provides strong vector based animation and XML web service integration.

2. **AJAX** (Asynchronous JavaScript and XML) – the combination of XML data, often through web services, and JavaScript code that allows data to be transferred to the server without the

requirement for page reload.

3. **WPF/E** (Windows Presentation Foundation Everywhere)
   – Microsoft technology that combines XAML and JavaScript
   to provide a rich interface.

These technologies allow the retailer to move away from providing the standard, *click-and-browse* interfaces to providing an experiential shopping journey. Great examples of rich interfaces in action include:

1. **Single page checkout**, using rich interface technology like AJAX to exchange data with the server without reloading the page, this enables the consumers to complete the checkout and payment process in one easy step.

2. **A search capability** built on rich interface technology like AJAX, would allow users to view results and sort the results in real-time without refreshing the page. Amazon uses this technology to build a rich interface to browse the inside of books and preview music CDs.

3. **A product configurator** built using rich interface technology like Flash to allow customers to configure products. An example would be designing their kitchen or their perfect car.

Today's rich interfaces provides us with more than just stunning visuals, this new technology allows the retailer to think out-of-the-box, to create a site that can closely resemble walking in to a store and even evolve this real-world experience. An example of shopping experience with these technologies could see the customer:

1. Enter a site and be welcomed with a personalised video of the latest offers

2. The customer wants to search for an item, and as they start typing into the search box results appear without them having to click the *Go* button.

3. The screen is then divided into two with the results shows in a toolbox, which can be moved around the screen, using the mouse the user can hover over any item in the toolbox and the second screen shows the item in full.

4. Once the user is happy to order the item they simply click buy and a window slides open, the new window lets the user know the item will be delivered in one day, along with the message, a small 10-second video is shown letting the user know of other items of interest.

5. The shopping basket is dynamic and if the user continues to add to the basket all items will be grouped, if they no longer add items to the basket the order is complete.

Rich interfaces are not limited to the online space, retailers can implement new technology to improve the in-store experience too. Bloomingdales, New York, have recently launched a new mirror that allows the user to super-impose the image of clothing items on to their reflection so the customer can get a feel of what items would look like without the need for trying them all on. The mirror also allows the user to send images and interact with friends and family who are at an internet point either at home or work.

It is important to remember that all customers are looking for a better experience. Shopping should be an enjoyable and the user of Rich interfaces allows the online retailer to create these experiences. Retailers should look at these technologies as enabling better business, but also note that they should only use technology to make improvements, and not just for the sake of technology. A good test for judging if a technology investment is worth making is if the Return on Investment (ROI) is realised within 6-12 months.

Customer Experience Management (CEM) - 5 Star Experience

Consumers want to be able to interact with a brand through any channel, when they pick up the phone or log on to the internet. They want to speak to someone who knows everything about the interactions between them and the company. This is what they expect as a bare minimum, but ultimately the customer is looking for a good customer experience. Rather than having to call the customer service department on non-delivery, just to be told *'I can see you placed an order with us, it is currently held at the warehouse waiting for dispatch'* information that a Customer Relationship Management (CRM) system delivers, they would rather have not had to place the call in the first place. Customers want to be told of any issues in advance and if an issue arises that the customer is not warned about in advance they should be compensated. Customers want a five star experience. If a customer orders room service in a five star hotel only to be told their food will not be delivered on time, it is more than likely the hotel will offer some type of explanation and do everything in their power to rectify the issue. If they were unable to rectify the issue, they will offer some form of concession. Customers are now expecting this five star service from every company they deal with. A recent Bain & Company survey found that only 8% of customers felt they were getting a superior service whilst 80% of companies felt they were delivering a superior service.

Retailers have amassed a considerable amount of data about the consumer, many also have a CRM system, a system that provides a single view into the customer, but what a CRM system does not record is the experience their customers have. Most retailers will conduct customer satisfaction surveys usually after an order has been placed however, this does not record the experience during the order or tell the retailer how to improve the experience.

The issue with deteriorating customer experience has magnified over the past few years, as customer expectations have risen primarily because of increased choice, great experience provided by very few retailers and improved Marketing/PR. With this the reputation of many retailers has grown, however the experience with them has not changed. This has led to an experience gap between the retailers offering and the expectations of the customer. The customers are expecting a service that is representative of the superior site or the great marketing. What is happening is that the Marketing/PR departments can kick in to overdrive and promote the retailer as being exceptional without looking at the experience the customer gets from them. A gap in the reputation of the company and the level of service they provide tends to harm the organisation. The retailer's reputation needs to be inline with the experience they offer and the expectations of the user.

The evolution of CRM is Customer Experience Management (CEM), the purpose of CEM is to monitor and track the experience a customer has with the retailer. Items that should be measured include:

1. Capture and distribute what a customer thinks about a company, rather than what the company knows about a

customer. The system should be available to everyone. This information can be captured using exit polls or surveys after an order has been fulfilled. Using a rating of 1-10 and a comments box.

2. Record events at touchpoints (calls, emails etc.) rather than after. Ask the consumer how they felt about the call and record the findings.

3. Surveys, targeted observations as apposed to post data click-throughs, look at the pathways and funnel analysis to determine if the customer is dropping out any point.

4. Business of leaders/product development consultants as apposed to customer service teams. Managing the overall experience is a strategic role and the data needs to be in the hands of someone who can control the direction of the company and make fundamental changes, if needed.

5. CEM systems locate positions to place advertising offerings in the gaps between expectations and experience. Experience management allows the retailer to spot the gaps by looking at survey data and areas where drop-off and exit rates are high.

CEM is more than just managing the experience of the consumer, it actively manages the reputation of the company, by distributing what the customers thinks and the experience the retailer is offering to everyone in the company. Data collection needs to be adopted to monitor the experience, we need to look at conversion rates from banners, retention rates, monitor how often a user has visited the *my account* section, or the number of calls users have made and report this data in single dashboard view so that senior managers can evaluate the overall customer experience levels.

It is important to remember that the customer's experience is based on their expectations and if you exceed their expectations you are offering them a better than expected experience, which will lead to improved profits. Managing expectations involves looking at your reputation, in the press, in your brand messaging and in your products. Retailers need to make sure what they are shouting about is what they can deliver. If there is a gap, they should reconsider the reputation they project or increase the experience to balance expectations.

5 Key Points to Engage 2.0

1. Customers are central to your business, allow them to control your offering, pass the ownership over to them.
2. Everything is about enhancing the customer experience - look at Up-Sell/Cross-Sell, Personalisation, Loyalty, RAI and Word-of-Mouth social tools to enhance it.
3. Getting search right is key in delivering a wonderful customer experience. Look at all the tools from contextual keywords search to guided navigation.
4. Green issues are now vital, be ethical, socially aware and environmental friendly.
5. Implement CEM tools to manage and monitor the customer experience.

Channel 2.0

Channel 2.0

Multi-channel retailing is defined as *operating a single retail organisation that has multiple touch points*, these touch points manifest in the form of:

1. **Call-centre operations**, where customers can use the telephone to interact with the retailer. Call-centres will usually be supported with offline advertising like a printed catalogue or direct response magazine advertisement.
2. **Physical store**, customers are able to walk into a store and interact with products and on-site customer service teams.
3. **By mail**, customers can submit orders using a form usually printed in a catalogue.
4. **Interactive TV**, using the television a customer can interact with a retailer to place an order.
5. **Internet**, the retailer's ecommerce site is usually the centre of any multi-channel strategy.
6. **Web services**, a new channel that allows customers to use any internet enabled device to communicate with the retailer.
7. **Kiosk,** an in-store touch-screen display that allows customers to buy items that are not readily available in that store.
8. **Mobile**, allowing purchasing and service requests/updates through a mobile phone.

A recent report by Gartner stated that 48% of retail organisations are looking to invest in improving their multi-channel offering this year. Many of these investments will involve launching an additional channel to support existing channels, whether it is a mail-order catalogue from a pure online retailer or an online offering from a clothing manufacturer. In addition, retailers are realising that ecommerce is significantly enhancing their other channels with over 65% of consumers researching a product online before purchasing it in-store.[9]

With a strategy based on delivering a next generation Channel 2.0 offering, retailers should be looking at synchronising the service level across all channels, these services should be fully integrated into the organisation and each channel should be correctly aligned across the following key mechanisms:

1. Pricing
2. Promotions
3. Gift Vouchers
4. Channel Interaction
5. Multi-channel marketing
6. Order fulfilment and returns

In addition, in this chapter we will look at the *single customer view*, *channels within channels* and consider *mobile as a channel* with special potential for the multi-channel retailer.

What are the considerations when devising a Channels 2.0 offering:

1. Listen to the consumer. Find out what they want from your offering. Most consumers want a single experience across all your channels.
2. Multi-channel is more than products just being available across all channels, it also involves opening up your offering to different markets. Let your consumers drive you to these markets (B2C companies moving to a B2B offering and vice versa).

3. Are all channels fully integrated and are they managed by a single team? Online, store, direct and emerging technology teams should be working within one department, creating a cohesive strategy.

4. Where does one channel enhance another? For instance online reservations for in-store collection, kiosks in-store or ecommerce support calls to the call-centre.

A recent Forrester report rated the whole industry with a 'C' in their understanding and approach to creating a true multi-channel environment. In this chapter, we will look at all the considerations that need to be factored in when creating a Channel 2.0 strategy for your organisation. By following these strategies, we can start to move the industry to receiving an 'A' grade during the next Forrester review.

Pricing in A Multi-Channel World

The Consumer Perspective

Consumers see one company with multiple channels and in this multi-channel world, they are looking for a single price across all channels. They want to be able to research a product online, walk into a store and pay the same price in-store as they saw online.

The Current Situation

Understandably, retailers have different costs per sale metric per channel, and to be competitive in each channel they will have created a different pricing model. This is especially true in the electronics market place where price comparison engines have driven margins to an all time low. Many retailers have combated the situation by launching channel specific brands to be able to offer low pricing on the web, and not interfere with their real brands multi-channel pricing. An example is Comet, a major UK electronics retailer, who has launched multiple white labelled versions of their site so they can compete with increasing online competition without driving margins down in their retail store. Another approach is to offer multiple pricing but provide a '*Web Price Matching*' service when customers walk in-store or buy over the telephone, this allows organisations to price individually for each channel but provide a single price to the multi-channel consumer.

The Channel 2.0 Model

In a Channel 2.0 model, the product needs to be separated from the service. Ultimately, pricing across any channel for a product should be the same and this is the only way to align pricing across all channels. Retailers need to look at unbundling services from the product, this allows them to push the product at a lower cost and drive additional revenues through high margin services. These services are usually unique to the company and therefore not included in downward price competition. Examples include:

1. Allowing customers to select delivery slots or pick up from a local store.
2. Providing in-store customers with independent customer service representatives, paid per hour to provide impartial advice.

However, a true Channel 2.0 model is not about aligning the price for a product across each channel but about aligning the price per customer across all channels. Every customer has a different value to the organisation and systems are currently available to offer variable pricing per user. This fights off the competition from the comparison engines, and avoids the customer having to experience conflicting pricing across the different channels whilst rewarding loyalty. Technology that allows price alignment per customer includes:

1. **Online** - Customers are recognised from previous visits. Pricing can be altered factoring loyalty and providing a greater discount for loyal customers.
2. **Mail-order/Telephone** - Customers are recognised from their name, email or postcode and can be provided different pricing on the telephone. Print on demand can provide exclusive prices per catalogue.
3. **In-store** - With electronic printers, which print out special vouchers from the consumer's loyalty card. The multi-channel retailer Tesco is currently offering this.

What happens to the price when marketing? When conducting any marketing exercise there is a cost with that exercise, marketing activities should be managed with promotion codes so they can be monitored effectively. Providing a promotion code per campaign, pricing can be altered at the marketing level. Ultimately, customers are looking for a single price across all channels, but this is a single price for them and not for all customers. With the right technology combined with a loyalty based pricing mechanism retailers can offer this and still maintain a healthy margin.

Promotions across Channels

The Consumer Perspective

Similar to pricing, customers are looking to receive similar promotions across all channels. If a customer receives an email with a *buy three get the cheapest free (3 for 2)* offer they want to be able to redeem that promotion in-store, online or on the phone. Customers also want an integrated loyalty scheme that is available across all channels. In the customer's mind they are always looking for value for money, this is the key. Customers are becoming aware of a range of different promotions and are able to cope with offers that are more complex. Promotions no longer need to be as simple as a discount, they can be *buy one get one free, get £10 off your next order, 3 for 2, buy DVD player get any DVD half price, buy 5 products for £30 or spend £50 save £10 on your next order.* The customers improved understanding is largely due to the increased exposure of such promotions.

The Current Situation

Some retailers are able to offer promotions across different channels. For example Boots the chemist, offers *3 for 2* on their vitamins both in-store and online. The reason many promotions are not available in multiple channels, is due to the complexities of the promotions and the capabilities of different disparate systems.

The Channel 2.0 Model

Running a *3 for 2* promotion on an ecommerce site may be simple, but this promotion capability needs replication across the call-centre and the point-of-sale (PoS) systems. A much easier approach would be to have a single promotions engine, either by having all channels running through a single system or by implementing a promotions engine that is utilised via web services across all systems. This would allow retailers to create multi-channel promotions and report on each . promotion across all channels.

Promotions are used for two very different purposes:
1. To provide the retailer the ability to promote specific products, with a discount, and increase sales. A very successful form of promotion is the *3 for 2*, this promotions drives up the average order value and it helps drive up sales of items in the promotion.
2. To allow the retailer to track the performance of multi-channel activities by tracking results against the promotions used. For example, a printed advert could run a promotion offer to customers with free shipping and to redeem the offer, customers will need to use the voucher code in-store, online or on the telephone. The retailer can then generate a report by promotion code to track the effectiveness of the campaign across channels.

Retailers need to look at implementing a promotions framework - to provide a system that is available across all channels. The promotions framework should provide the following features and capabilities:
1. Allowing a single promotion to be redeemed across any channel.
2. The ability to report on a single promotion regardless of channel utilised.
3. Store the receptiveness of each consumer to a particular kind of promotion i.e. this consumer prefers *3 for 2* offers rather than *buy 1 get 1 free* offers.
4. Store additional channel specific data, such as recordings

of the emotional experience a customer had in the offline retail store or the conversion rate for the online use of the promotion.

To enable such a framework, retailers have three options:

1. Build similar capabilities on all systems - call-centre, online and mail-order systems should all be able to provide the same promotion. Promotions then need to be synchronised between systems.
2. Have a single multi-channel system for all transactions.
3. Create a web services framework that allows a single promotions engine to be deployed across all systems.

Promotions play an important role in the retailers' world. The correct strategy can help boost sales and improve the overall flexibility of the company. To implement the right strategy retailers need to be able to create the right promotions in a timely manner with the ability to report on the performance of any promotion in real-time. Tools are now available to allow the retailer to create technically complex promotions using a structured framework but most companies have yet to deliver these from a single system.

Gift Vouchers

The Consumer Perspective

Customers love the idea of gift vouchers. They are perfect, as presents get even harder to find for friends and family. Customers want to be able to buy vouchers from various channels and they either want them delivered to themselves or directly to the recipient, as a physical gift card or electronically delivered codes.

Current Situation

Customers are daunted by the current situation where most in-store vouchers cannot be redeemed online and online vouchers cannot be redeemed in-store. Gift cards by credit card companies are great for the consumer but provide little benefit to the retailer.

The Channel 2.0 Model

To make vouchers work through multiple channels they need to be integrated into multiple systems. The primary considerations for an ideal voucher process including purchase, delivery, redemption and security.

Purchase

A voucher should be available for purchase, through any channel from mobile to in-store for a variable value, which can be either a physical gift card or a virtual code for redemption. In-store kiosk or checkout staff could take email or mobile number to instantly deliver a voucher.

Delivery

A voucher can be delivered electronically as a code number by email or mobile or even just written down. The second option is for the voucher to be distributed as a gift card. These are normally plastic cards and can be customised with personal photographs.

Redemption

The electronic code number is entered online on a payment page, used in-store by the sales clerk entering it into the PoS system or redeemed via a call-centre. A gift card would have a magnetic stripe or smartchip that would allow it to be scanned into a PoS terminal, which would save the need to key in a code.

Security

Security is a major concern with gift cards but this is alleviated by:

1. Card and code activation only on sale, which reduces the risk of cards being stolen or codes being guessed.
2. Using just eight digit alphanumeric codes would give over two trillion codes.
3. Security can be increased by allowing the optional creation of passwords, pins or specific allocation so that only a particular email address can redeem the voucher. As these would not be written down, they would prevent a card being used even if it was stolen.

Gift vouchers are in strong demand by the consumer and in a Channel 2.0 model it is essential that a fully channel independent solution is available.

Channel Interaction

The Consumer Perspective

In a multi-channel environment, consumers are looking for an experience that allows them to interact seamlessly with the retailer regardless of channel. Examples include:

1. Researching a product online and reserving it for collection at a local store.
2. Purchasing a product in-store and returning it via an online returns management system.
3. Purchasing a product on-line and returning or exchanging it

in-store.

4. Ordering an item in-store for delivery and tracking the order online.

5. Buying a voucher online and redeeming it on the telephone.

The list can go on and the pattern that emerges is that consumers want to be able to choose the way they interact with the retailer and not be restricted by their choice of channel.

The Current Situation

The majority of retailers are now evenly represented across all channels, with the top-tier retailers moving in the right direction by starting to provide simple integrated offerings. Argos is probably the leader with the introduction of reserve online and pick-up in-store. However, there is still a majority of retailers that continue to operate each channel independently, treating each additional channel as an extra physical store and creating new systems and processes, which are channel specific. This lack of strategic input builds roadblocks and bottlenecks when retailers start to consider providing an integrated offering.

The Channel 2.0 Model

The consumer who interacts with a retailer across multiple channels both spends more and is more loyal, so it is more important than ever to get the channel interaction correct. With Channel 2.0, organisations need to look at the overall system architecture, making sure there is either a single system in place to manage all orders and customer information, or that all systems are built in to a Service Orientated Architecture (SOA) standard allowing systems to integrate tightly together. Once the overall technical mindset is in place, creating an integrated offering becomes a simpler task. The essential technology requirements for a Channel 2.0 model are:

A single order system provides a huge number of benefits for customers. Retailers should start to provide a fully integrated approach, allowing consumers to walk into a store to trace an order and pick it up if it has not been dispatched. For the retailer it also provides a number of opportunities, if an item is out of stock in the central warehouse when a customer places an order, the retailer could check local stores and direct the customer to pick up part of their order from the store. In a single order system model, consumers will also start to receive a greater level of service.

A single customer database provides the ability for channels to provide a personalised service to the consumer. If a customer places an in-store order, they can be emailed an offer based on that purchase. This removes the duplication of customer records across channels and helps the retailer really understand whom their customers are and how they are interacting. In addition, the single customer database ensures that marketing messages for each channel are synchronised so that a customer never gets too many or even worse conflicting messages. This single customer database would allow a customer to walk into the store looking for a cartridge replacement for the printer they bought online and an in-store assistant could check the customer's previous order history to locate the correct printer cartridge.

In the Channel 2.0 environment, the customer is in the middle and to support that customer, data needs to be shared across all channels, either by creating a single environment or by integrating systems together. The complexity of this task may be the reason why many retailers have not yet integrated there systems. However, a recent Forrester study estimated that 45% of retailers are looking at overhauling their IT infrastructure. A single system that provides a single view of customers, orders, returns and promotions should be a strong focus in any new system deployment.

Multi-channel marketing

Customer Perspective

The customer sees advertising on various different channels for a company and he/she believes the advertising is for a single company irrespective of channel. The customer chooses the channel that is most appropriate to them, so when they see a TV advertisement for an electrical retailer the fact that it contains a web site address and the address of the retail stores, makes it apparent that these channels are open to them. However, when the customer sees a marketing message online and is directed to a web site, at that point they see if other channel options are available for that company. If they don't see other channel options they are most likely to select the ecommerce site as a channel. However, if they are committed to making a purchase in-store after researching a product and getting advice and the channel options are not obvious they may consider going elsewhere.

Current Situation

Currently, retailers' different channels are often run by different departments, which vie for space on marketing communication like email. Most marketing communications include information on all the channel options available to the consumer. Many multi-channel retailers make the misconception that all forms of online marketing from email to search are there to encourage online sales through the ecommerce site.

The Channel 2.0 Model

Once retailers are managed by a single team and customer information is stored in a single system, the goal to convert a customer to purchase becomes much easier. The reality is that each channel enhances others. As covered in the Marketing 2.0 chapter of this book, marketing is about influencing the customer behaviour through their buying cycle. Therefore, marketing communications should be implemented in a manner that is most appropriate at trigger points in the customer's buying cycle irrespective of the marketing media that is used. This means that if email marketing is seen as an ideal choice to influence customer behaviour to encourage store visits then it should be used, just as it is currently used to improve online sales. This applies to every media including search and banner advertising.

Order fulfilment and returns

Customer Perspective

A customer wants to buy all available products from every channel and when the order is dispatched, they want to receive it in a timely fashion. The customer also wants to return and exchange products through their preferred channel.

Current Situation

Retailers have the biggest problem managing logistics and distribution for their retail stores and their online operations. Warehouses are often split to separate stock for stores and online activity and products are distributed on a demand-driven approach. The logistics of managing in-store refunds and returns for online offerings has been difficult even though this is an area of clear advantage for multi-channel retailers.

The Channel 2.0 Model

The theory is much simpler than the implementation, particularly due to disparate systems but becomes a lot easier with a single system. Stock for distribution across channels from retail, mail-order and web should be stored and monitored in a single place. The allocation of stock should happen in real-time so that a customer is never disappointed and there is no chance of a single item being allocated twice. When a customer orders items that are not available through a central distribution channel, they should automatically be shipped from a local store, which has the item in-stock or if they prefer, they should be able to collect at the local store.

Stock allocation and distribution should use predictive analysis tools that look at demand and trends to ensure that products are always available to the customer.

A single database will ensure that returns can be made through any channel. When a customer buys online, they should be able to take an item back in-store and return or exchange it just as they would an item they had purchased in-store. An in-store purchase should also be able to be returned online just by logging in to a self-service area on the web site and making a return request.

One Customer, Multiple Channels

In order for retailers to provide good customer service, they need to access to all the information stored about a customer, available at a touch of button regardless of which interface they may be using. It is not only the retailer who needs this data but also the customer. Providing the customer with the ability to self-serve so they are able to retrieve relevant information from you without having to speak to a real person can help both the retailer, by reducing customer service costs, and the customer, by allowing them to quickly tap into information they need at a touch of button. For example, Fed-Ex always stores the tracking information on their parcels, so in order to cut back on customer service calls they allowed the customer track parcels themselves. Taking a look at the top five most common requests, which account for 92% of all inbound request made via email or telephone to a customer service team, we can start to identify ways to extract data from internal systems and make that data available directly to the customer and hence reduce the number of inbound requests:

Problem with an order (either not received or damaged in transit)	An online order management system, which allows the customer to view all recent orders and check the progress of the order. The online system should show expected delivery dates and display all the information the internal systems have about the order. Instead of showing, order *waiting* or *dispatched* it could say, full order expected to be dispatched in 2 days (waiting for item 3 of the order which is due in 2 days).
Change an order, or alter personal records	Using the same order management as above, customers are able to locate an order, and change the items in the order. This would be based on rules, so if the order has already been dispatched the customer is provided details of how to return the order, if the order has not been dispatched they are provided with the ability to change or cancel line items.

To return an item (Return rates with apparel average 14%)	Customers want the ability to easily return items, if they purchase an item in-store they want to be able to return the item online and vice versa. All systems should be aware of the order placed. Customers want to use any channel to start the returns process. Ideally, they want to be able to return items without having to speak to a customer services member. A good implementation of a returns systems would be, returns kiosks that can provide the customer with the ability to authorise returns and then enable them to drop the item at a counter and be refunded online.
Clarification about a product/ service	There are a number of questions customers will have about a product, questions which product information alone cannot answer. These questions are usually common across channels. Questions such as *'does this microwave fit in a Moben kitchen unit?'* are difficult to answer but a good starting point is to have a single knowledge base of all questions and the answers to those questions. Answers can be created by customer service teams, manufacturers or the other customers through forums, wikis and reviews. This knowledge base is then opened up to the customer and all staff regardless of the channel. Therefore, a question answered online is also available to customers contacting the call-centre.
To make a complaint	Complaints should be encouraged. Many customers will tend to shy away from making complaints to a human and would much prefer to submit a complaint anonymously. Other times an item might be so cheap that when it fails it is not worth returning, leaving a disappointed customer with no feedback to the retailer. There is no doubt that in certain situations that a human response is required to handle complaints, but opening up the doors to candid feedback from the consumer can help the company learn from the customers. These complaints should be added to a complaints management system and each one should be looked at to see if an improvement could be made.

Retailers are moving towards a single database to store all customer interactions, which provides a single view of the customer so that retailers are able to understand the buying habits of valuable customers and support their needs effectively. The multi-channel customer wants to interact with the retailer across all channels and they will reward the retailer with their loyalty in return, but how does the retailer get there. It can be very expensive and resource intensive to throw out existing systems and implement a single system that operates across all channels, the solution lies in taking relevant data from multiple systems and representing this data via a reporting interface. By using web services or other forms of data extraction, retailers can use the new solutions provided by companies such as Microsoft (SQL Server 2005 Analysis Services) and get a single view across the customer through an interface that spans multiple systems. Once they have this view, retailers can look across all channels and use data to create effective campaigns, based on purchasing patterns across a multi-channel environment.

We have stated that in the Web 2.0 environment, a single database is not vital, but a single view into the customer is. With the advent of the service orientated architecture, web services retailers will be able to tap into every database in the company and analyse the data in a new way that will enable them to create multi-channel campaigns and allow the customer to interact with the retailer across any channel.

Mobile Consumers

The mobile market provides the greatest opportunity of any channel, globally more customers have mobiles than any other internet-connected device and as new mobile devices with better interfaces enter the market place, customers will increase the usage of this channel for their interactions with retailers. Email was one of the first major developments of the internet and it is also the first major application for the mobile internet, almost every major organisation has a workforce of email-connected users, who are able to pick up and answer emails 24 hours a day. As the internet moves from the desktop to the mobile, there will be users who will want to interact with retailers in new and exciting ways using their mobiles devices. Some great examples include:

1. **Real time delivery checking** - One of the biggest issues with ecommerce orders is trying to provide an exact time for the delivery of the order, so that users can ensure they are available to accept the order, especially with orders that will not fit through the standard letter box. With a internet enabled mobile device, and a web services connected ecommerce store, customers will be able to track the progress of delivery to their door-step, so they can be *out and about* and arrive back home in time to accept the delivery.

2. **Location based services** - There are already a number of services that allow consumers to buy products online, through their mobiles but these experiences do not fully exploit the capabilities of location-based services. Location based services allow the mobile site operator to know the geographical location of the customer. The ability to locate a customer's whereabouts whilst they are browsing your

mobile site, could allow you to direct them to their closest store and notify the customer service team of the expected arrival, leaving the customer experiences fully integrated from mobile touch points to in-store touch points.

3. **Mobile marketing** - The mobile is an always-on device, providing the retailer with the ability to market consumers in a new and exciting ways. Knowing the customer is likely to receive the message immediately, allows a retailer to communicate with them at any time. For example, a customer can be sent an email as soon as they leave a store, with or without making a purchase.

In 2008 when mobile internet is expected to reach critical mass, customers will be placing even more demands on the retailer. The customer will always be connected to the internet, and they will want retailers to step up their offering and systems to enable the retailers operations through the mobile channel.

With the majority of internet enabled mobiles, operating on a clunky interface and slow connection, retailers have paid little attention to the mobile channel, very few have any form of mobile offering. This is due to change, the number of internet enabled mobile devices is set to out-grow desktop PC's in 2010, this will lead to a change in the way customers deal with organisations. The existing mobile infrastructure is new and there is no common platform at present. If a retailer wishes to launch a mobile offering they will need to test on multiple devices and the differences between the systems are vast. However, a common platform is in development and should be realised in the first quarter of 2008, this will lead to a rapid increase in the number of users and provide retailers with an easier platform to launch through. With this in mind, retailers should not wait until 2008 to take advantage of the capabilities of the mobile channel. A good starting point is for retailers to start collecting information about a customer's mobile capability. When a customer registers, ask for their mobile telephone number and ask if they the customer have an internet/email enabled mobile phone. With this information, start engaging with the customer through their mobile, for example, using SMS notification to alert users when an order has been dispatched. Start an early dialogue through the customer's mobile phone with technology currently available and introduce new mobile services as they become viable.

Channels within Channels

Channels are rapidly intertwining with each other to provide an integrated experience, successful examples include:

1. **Catalogues in retail store**. Argos have implemented a successful model to allow customers to browse in the comfort of their own home and then use the same catalogue in-store to make a purchase and take the item home immediately.

2. **In-store kiosks**. Mothercare have been using Kiosks to in smaller stores to allow customers the ability to order items, which are not held at the smaller stores. This enables them to offer their full range of products across all stores regardless of size. Customers can place orders on the kiosk and collect in-store at a convenient time.

3. **Print catalogues viewed online**. Many online retailers are using rich technology to allow the customer to view a printed catalogue online, providing the time-tested experience of browsing through a catalogue but online with hyperlinked products that go directly to the buy pages.

As demonstrated in the first two examples above, there are benefits to providing integrated channels to the consumers but these should only be implemented if they add real value to the experience. To determine if channel integration will be successful retailers need to understand the benefits. In the first example above, we can see the benefit of catalogue shopping in-store, it enables the customer to get an item immediately without having to wait for delivery. In the second example, Mothercare have allowed smaller stores to carry the full range of products, so the customer can order everything in one trip without having to travel to a larger out-of-town store. However, in the third example it is difficult to see the real benefit of the channel integration, as the customer is provided with a simple catalogue on an advanced device and the retailer could effectively be missing valuable dynamic merchandising opportunities. Retailers need to look at the real benefits of channel integration and only implement a solution if it improves the customers single channel experience.

As new channels develop (specifically mobile and other portable internet enabled devices), channel integration will be in the control of the customer. The great worry with this advent of new technology is that customers have the ability to locate lower prices or cheaper alternatives at a touch of a button, commoditising the products. For example, if a customers walks in to a store with their mobile device and they get the feel of a particular product, look for the cheapest price on their mobile and place an order on the competitor's mobile site there and then or maybe later. The retail store gained nothing and the competitor benefited from a sale. To avoid situations such as this, retailers need to look at implementing the strategies such as:

1. Understand the channel integration and provide the customer with special promotion codes to use on their mobile device,

actively cannibalising one channel for another.

2. Bundle accessories so products cannot be price matched.
3. Provide value added services like Plasma TV installation.
4. Actively target these price-checking customers with a price match.
5. Create a dual channel experience, to allow the customer to use their mobile to enable a social shopping experience sending information to friends or family.

Retailers need to look at the way customers want to interact with them, and improve the touch points to allow the customer to interact the way they want to. The customer is taking ownership of the relationship and retailers need to make sure they are available when the customer wants them to be.

5 Key Points for Channel 2.0

1. Look at it from the customer's point of view, all new channel launches should bring value to your overall proposition. Place the customer in the middle and let them choose the way they interact with you.
2. Develop a single system for promotions, customers and orders. If you cannot do this, tightly integrate and make sure data flows freely between systems.
3. Look at orders and returns across multiple channels – this creates real value for the multi-channel retailer.
4. Ask yourself - could kiosks be the answer for managing big-item orders in-store and returns?
5. Start collecting intelligence about your customer's mobile capability now, and use the existing technology to start early dialogue through the mobile.

Conclusion

Ecommerce 2.0 discusses the evolution of customer interaction with companies, and the continuous relationships they build with brands. Engaging with a customer has advanced, subsequent to which, the implementation of unique marketing campaigns is required in order to guide the consumer to multiple touch-points.

Within this book, we have provided you with the same knowledge that has enabled companies to utilise premium data and technologies to deliver successful campaigns that ultimately, have built profitable businesses. Companies who move towards grasping these new practises and implementing them, will undoubtedly benefit from this knowledge.

As the principles of Imano, we have over 10 years professional experience in delivering profitable campaigns for some of the largest and most successful companies in the world. Our goal, is to aid in the effective implementation of these special techniques and to ensure real business value is provided through Ecommerce 2.0 solutions and Marketing 2.0 campaigns.

References

References

1. US Online Marketing Forecast: 2005 To 2010
Dollars Will Follow Consumers Online, Driving Spending To $26 Billion By 2010
Publication Date: 2 May 2005
Authors: Charlene Li, Shar VanBoskirk
Forrester Research, Inc
http://www.forrester.com/Research/Document/Excerpt/0,7211,36546,00.html

Left Brain Marketing Planning
Publication Date: 16 May 2005
Authors: Shar VanBoskirk Chris Charron, Gregory N. Flemming, Ph.D., Tenley McHarg
Forrester Research, Inc
http://www.forrester.com/Research/Document/Excerpt/0,7211,36427,00.html

2.Getting the Most Out of All Your Customers
Publication Date: 1 Jul 2004
Authors: Jacquelyn S. Thomas, Werner Reinartz, V. Kumar
Harvard Business Review
www.hbr.org

3.The One Number You Need to Grow
Publication Date: 2 Dec 2003
Authors: Frederick F. Reicheld
Harvard Business Review
www.hbr.org

4. The Long-term Impact of Promotion and Advertising on Consumer Brand Choice

Publication Date: 1996

Authors: F. Mela, Sunil Gupta, and Donald R. Lehmann, 1996 [96-127]

Marketing Science Institute

http://www.msi.org/publications/publication.cfm?pub=445

5. DoubleClick's Touchpoints II: The Changing Purchase Process

Publication Date: March 2004

Doubleclick

6. Cross Media Optimization Studies (XMOS)

Interactive Advertising Bureau

http://www.iab.net/xmos/case.asp

7. How Damaging Are Negative Customer Reviews?

Publication Date: 10 January 2007

Authors: Sucharita Mulpuru

Forrester Research, Inc

http://www.forrester.com/Research/Document/Excerpt/0,7211,40649,00.html

8. Brand Magic: Harry Potter Marketing

Publication Date: February 2007

Authors: Frédéric Dalsace, Coralie Damay, and David Dubois

Harvard Business Review

www.hbr.co.uk

9. Which Retailers Offer The Best Cross-Channel Customer Experience?
Multichannel Retailing Best Practices
Publication Date: September 15, 2004
Authors: Carrie A. Johnson
Forrester Research, Inc
http://www.forrester.com/Research/Document/Excerpt/0,7211,34575,00.html